THE ANVIL OF SCOTTISH HISTORY

Stories of Stirling

Murray Cook

The Anvil of Scottish History: Stories of Stirling by Murray Cook.

First edition published in Great Britain in 2020 by Extremis Publishing Ltd., Suite 218, Castle House, 1 Baker Street, Stirling, FK8 1AL, United Kingdom. *www.extremispublishing.com*

Extremis Publishing is a Private Limited Company registered in Scotland (SC509983) whose Registered Office is Suite 218, Castle House, 1 Baker Street, Stirling, FK8 1AL, United Kingdom.

A CIP catalogue record for this book is available from the British Library.

ISBN: 978-1-9996962-5-2

Typeset in Goudy Bookletter 1911, designed by The League of Moveable Type.
Printed and bound in Great Britain by IngramSpark, Chapter House, Pitfield, Kiln Farm, Milton Keynes, MK11 3LW, United Kingdom.

Front cover artwork is Copyright © Aleks Safronov at Shutterstock.
Back cover artwork by Shelley Murray from Pixabay.
Cover design and book design is Copyright © Thomas A. Christie.
Incidental vector artwork from Pixabay.

Author image and internal photographic images are Copyright © Murray Cook and are sourced from the author's private collection, unless otherwise stated. Please refer to the Acknowledgements section for a full listing of other incorporated photographic imagery.

This book is dedicated to my three wonderful daughters:

Kirsty, Eilidh and Heather

Contents

THE ANVIL OF SCOTTISH HISTORY

STORIES OF STIRLING

Introduction

FOR those that don't know me, I have the very great privilege and pleasure to be Stirling Council's archaeologist. At the retirement of my colleague Dr Elspeth King, the former Director of The Smith Museum and Art Gallery, I was greatly honoured to be asked to take over her weekly column for the local paper, the *Stirling Observer*. The articles delve into my digs, ancient objects, wee mysteries and overlooked things, and I hope that they are funny and light in tone – but if you disagree, then this is perhaps not the book for you.

The articles are confined to around 300 words, so there's always something more I could have said or a topic to revisit. I always had an idea that I would perhaps one day publish them, but as my publisher pointed out – why would anyone want to read something that had already been printed? I asked him whether he wasn't meant to be on my side, but he replied with an enigmatic smile and a shrug of his shoulders. Hmm... I wondered if Neil Oliver has to deal with this sort of thing. But then I pondered a little more... perhaps an expansion of the columns could form a history of Scotland as seen through the lens of Stirling? Of course, such a history would encompass what I imagine you'd be interested in, so you'd have to trust me.

But why would anyone want to read about Stirling? It's a pokey wee place (if you know how, it's possible to walk from the city centre to the edge in 10 minutes) which, while technically a city thanks to the Queen, has a smaller population than many big towns. Or indeed, why would you read about it again when you may have already read my first book?

The reason is, of course, that Stirling – apart from being amazingly beautiful – sits at the lowest crossing point of the River Forth. This means that every army that ever invaded or resisted invasion had to cross the river at Stirling. So, for the last 2000 years, blood and treasure were lost and heroes and villains created in perpetual struggle for control of this key location. This means that almost every single aspect of Scotland's history either impacts, or is impacted by, this wonderful wee place.

Stirling was Scotland's ancient capital and remains its best preserved medieval city with the best preserved city walls and late medieval hospital, the oldest and best preserved royal park, as well as one of the best preserved Renaissance palaces in Europe. It is home to the world's oldest football and curling stone – and the home of tartan. Stirling was the grounds for the two most important battles in Scottish history as well as having fought Romans, Angles,

Picts, Vikings, the English, other Scots, Cromwell, Jacobites and the Hanoverians, and played a key role in the preparations for D-Day. It is the place where our identity and indeed our very existence has been forged and repeatedly tested: the anvil of Scottish history.

Nowhere else in Europe can you walk in 30 minutes from a medieval castle to a Celtic fort to a medieval battlefield and back to spot where Bonnie Prince Charlie stood. Stirling is absolutely awesome, and those that live and work here should never forget it. But why, I hear you cry, if Stirling is so important is it so small? The reason is the slow, inevitable grind of UK history, as Scotland was formed from lots of smaller older, now-lost kingdoms so too was the UK from Scotland, England, Wales and Northern Ireland. At the start of 17th century a Scottish king (James VI) became the English king (James I), and Stirling went from being a very important place in an independent Scotland to a small parochial backwater in a much bigger UK. As we shall see, there was a second wave of investment in the 19th and early 20th centuries when Glasgow merchants, who were making money from the British Empire, chose to move out of the city to Stirling (amongst lots of other places) and Stirling became one of the richest places in the world.

So while the book is mostly organised chronologically, it does bob and weave a little. This rich and complex history requires some patience to untangle. The past lies thick here; it 'pools, flows, rushes, slows' and when you walk our streets, your feet join thousands of others over the millennia. So please bear with me – a story about World War II could lead to the 17th century plague, and Robert The Bruce features in the discovery of the world's oldest curling stone – to make things clearer I've added a series of grid references and longitudes and latitudes, but I hope the details will prove entertaining rather than confusing.

Dig for Victory (or really for fun)

Archaeology, as well as being a big Greek word designed to impress (but really all it does is intimidate and confuse), is the study of the past through the objects our ancestors left behind. It is a highly tangible link to those who came before us, and it is their legacy to us. This is your past and, because of this, I try to do as many free digs as possible. I want people to be involved, but it's not exactly just a walk in the park! Let me take you to a Saturday morning in September 2019...

So, what exactly would drive eight otherwise sane and well-balanced adults, registered voters one and all, to climb through tick-ridden bracken, tripping over treacherous bramble tentacles and slipping and sliding over scabby dead branches up a misty hill to spend all day on their hands and knees furiously scraping at the cold, clammy and unyielding soil of Stirling? And why would they come back for more?

These questions ran through my mind as I struggled up Scout Head near Gargunnock with eight brave and hardy volunteers to explore Baston Burn, a 2000 year old roundhouse with 3m thick walls, a structural form probably related to brochs. And yet, if you have to ask, you will never know and certainly never understand.

Archaeology is not glamorous, and it's certainly nothing like Indiana Jones (although he's clearly of Scottish descent on his father's side). We rarely find gold or treasure, but they are no match for the real thrill: exploring the unknown; revealing things that no one has seen for millennia; contributing to the sum total of human knowledge; a shared aim with like-minded people. Not to mention new friends, bad jokes, soggy biscuits, lukewarm coffee, the warm glow of sweat from a day's honest labour and the aches that remind you that you did something different today.

So have I sold you on it, or are you convinced that I'm not right in the head? The clincher either way is probably the following picture of what we uncovered after 20 hours of toil: the face of the wall, not seen for 2000 years – all of which was then duly covered up again. So, was it worth it? If it's too much or indeed too little a return, don't worry, just keep reading the *Stirling Observer* and I'll keep you posted. But if it's sparked something in your soul, an itch you cannot scratch, please look me up!

The thrill of discovery: a 2000 year old wall

Chapter One

Beginnings: 360 Million BC to AD 70

How old is time? An excursion into geology

No, really, how old is it? Don't worry; you've not strayed into a book on philosophy. In the past, people thought the biblical version of creation was literally true. It was calculated that the earth was around 6,000 years old by adding the ages of people from Adam and Eve up to Christ. All this changed during the

Views of main landforms

Scottish Enlightenment, one of the great world's greatest intellectual move-ments, when a Scot called James Hutton discovered deep geological time in around 1760. That makes time as we know it today about 259 years old.

Stirling's incredible geology

Obviously the landscape is far older than that, and the scale of geological time is mindboggling. Stirling's Castle Rock, Craigforth and Abbey Craig are all vol-canic, formed from 400 million year old intrusive flows of magma. Scorching flows of lava spread across where the Forth would be and flowed down the northern side of the Ochils sealing fossil beds and layers and layers of coal, these having formed when Scotland lay at the equator in warm shallow seas. Frag-ments of these fossils turn up from time to time where people have quarried and dug. But if you really want to see a fossilised sea bed, walk up the Bannockburn to Swallowhaugh (274575, 687674; 56° 03' 55" N 4° 00' 58" W) where it has carved through the geological strata to the underlying fossilised shell beds – it is absolutely astonishing.

The oldest life in Stirling

Around 360-260 million years ago Stirling sat in the middle of a rift valley. The line of the fault is the south-facing scarp of the Ochils and the area where the Forth now flows drops by 3-5km, all of which was sealed during the ice age. The fault is still active and every few years there is an earthquake, though very small – just enough to wake people up in the night.

This rugged landscape was in turn buried by tonnes of ice. There was at least 1km of glacier above our fair city, grinding, crushing and pushing. Indeed, the ice was so heavy that it depressed all of Scotland (a bit like the foot-ball/rugby results), and we're still recovering – while you read this piece you have become slightly higher, thanks to a process called isostatic bounce. The last of the ice melted 10,000 years ago, which created the moraines at Callander (well worth a look). This melted ice filled the Lake of Menteith and indeed the whole of the Forth Valley. This vast lost sea slowly drained as Scotland bounced back, becoming a bog so people could only live on the high ground.

Crinoid

Sometimes, if not dry, it was just enough to stop the farm being washed away, so we get Falleninch, or Inchie or Inch of Leckie (derived from the Gaelic 'innis' for island, or, in this case, just slightly higher ground). Thus all the old places in Stirling are on the high ground (Stirling, Dunblane, Cowie and Kippen), while the new ones are all on the low ground (Raploch, Cornton and Plean).

The awesome might of glaciers

Anyway, this diversion into geology was to show you what I uncovered in July 2019 when digging a 2,000 year old fort in the King's Park. I thought at first these were tool marks from gouging out the rock for a defensive ditch, but they went into the sands and gravels, so they couldn't be archaeology. In Scotland all the sands and gravels date to after the last ice age. So these marks were caused by something huge and lumbering and over 10,000 years old.[1] I think this is the scouring of the King's Park's solid geology by a glacier, the same one that smoothed out Dumyat. Now while I am not a bible literalist, or a practising Christian even, I can find the divine in such a majestic process.

Glacier mark

Our earliest ancestors had a whale of a time: 10,000 to 7,000 BC

The coastline of this lost sea (which people until at least the 13th century still thought existed, and called it the Sea of Scotland) is still visible today. You can see its coastline at the King's Knot, Abbey Craig, Blair Drummond, Balquhid-

---

[1]   No, it's not one of my jokes!

derock, just above Gargunnock and below Thornhill and Kippen. Just stop and look – if you travel west from Stirling you drop down onto the Carse and if you look north or south it's all flat, a vast great plain: a lost sea bed.

And of course where there is a sea, there is a tide and something to eat: crabs, mussels, limpets, cockles, seaweed, wading birds, deer eating the seaweed and the odd beached whale. There were people in Scotland before the ice retreated, because there was always something to eat in the sea; all you had to do was follow the coast. We were just like any other animal. For hundreds and thousands of years we bred and we spread, our clever fingers and brains figuring out how to survive. We moved from the African plains to the Mediterranean, then to Spain, France, England and then finally Scotland. These, our earliest ancestors, followed resources into the hills during the summer and then went back to the coast in the winter. We don't know their names or what language they spoke; their lives were '*nasty, brutish and short*'. Most would die in their twenties due to the harshness of life at the time: a cut or an infection could be fatal, bears and other predators hunted them as they hunted deer, and child birth was incredibly risky. But they survived and prospered, and eventually led to us.

All along this lost coast are the slight fragmentary evidences of our earliest ancestors from a period called the Mesolithic. Tiny bits of sharp, glass-like grey stone called chert on the high ground denote the remains of their camps. They are the ultimate needle in a haystack, and I think I have identified three or four possibilities over the last 10 years: next to the King's Knot, Gargunnock and Kippen.

Rock shelter

The earliest evidence for people in Stirling

Unlike most of our ancestors' tools, chert survives in the damp Scottish ground. But it takes a special set of circumstances to preserve organic material. You remember I mentioned that the inland sea gradually drained and became a bog? Well, this bog was full of peat – which preserves bone. While peat was being cleared for centuries (more about that later on), the scale of clearance really ramped up during the late 18th and 19th centuries as landowners tried to squeeze more money from their land. This process uncovered at least four whale skeletons around Stirling, and one of the best preserved was at Woodyett Farm on the Meiklewood estate at Gargunnock, which was run by the Graham family. These chaps had their own very impressive burial lair in Gargunnock kirk (270708, 694316; 56° 07′ 26″ N 4° 04′ 53″ W).[2]

What a brilliant name Meiklewood is. Say it again and let it roll round your tongue. It means big wood, presumably a medieval reference to when there were far more trees. That wood is there again in Woodyett (Wood Yett, or Gate), another great Scots word. Anyway, the current Meiklewood house is still standing and was built by Colonel David Graham in the early 1800s. The Colonel also built the road bridge we all use when we cross the Forth from Gargunnock to Blair Drummond and, believe it or not, several dozen families lived on this road in the middle of the bog when it was being cleared for cultivation.

The Grahams of Meiklewood

Drainage works in the 1870s at Woodyett uncovered the skull and skeleton of a Rorqual whale, a classification that covers several species which range in size from nine tonnes to 120 tonnes. The Smith Museum and Art Gallery contains some of the bones, and they look to me like a smaller species. Looking in detail at these bones you can see a series of gouges in them. These are tool marks and, while some of them may be from the workers who uncovered the skeleton, it's likely that most will be from our Mesolithic ancestors hacking and carving the whale's flesh, preparing an enormous feast – so enormous that they couldn't possibly eat it all before it started to rot. We know this because one of them lost their tool:

Stirling's earliest meal

---

2   Tours of which are provided by the local community.

a roughly 7,000 year old red deer antler beam mattock, currently on display in National Museum of Scotland in Edinburgh. The Smith Museum and Art Gallery has some similar examples. Presumably, this whale butchering would have happened fairly regularly, but what did our ancestors think these whales were?

Silenced and forgotten: generation upon generation: 7000 to 1000 BC

Several thousand generations lie between us and the people who carved up the Woodyett whale. They left us very little: some stray mute objects and the odd standing stone. In the Neolithic, our ancestors adopted farming brought by immigrants across Europe from close to what is now Syria and Iraq. All of them already literate and numerate while we, as my Dad would've said, were still running around with our bottoms painted blue. Anyway, some of the unexpected consequences of farming were bad, broken and sore backs (from manual lifting), poor teeth (from all the grit in the bread), rats and vermin (because we stayed in one place), and lots more spare time. The spare time came between planting and harvesting – people dreamed and planned and organised. We started to build, and build big. Very little of these buildings survive, as they were built from wood – all of which has gone and rotted. But the wood they used, mostly oak, was incredible: ancient, massive looming trees, carved from the lost Caledonian Forest. These trees have no modern equivalent, they are all gone, though perhaps the medieval trees at Dalkeith Country Park come close. But imagine thousands of them. Imagine Scotland like the Amazon rainforest: a vast green lung swaying with the breeze. Stirling's biggest Neolithic building lay under what is now a rather nondescript 1980s street: Ochilmount (281622, 690335; 56° 05' 28" N 3° 54' 15" W). It comprised two massive enclosures, which we call cursuses, built of individual posts. The biggest of the enclosures was 27m wide and 50m long.

They were built around 5,000 years ago and, while we're not really sure what for, the most likely explanation is for religious processions at key times of the year. There was presumably something at one end, but whatever it was is long gone, as have the names of the gods or goddesses and the music and detail of their rituals. However, we can glimpse something fragmentary but very important: each cursus was a fence, a boundary. This means that access could be controlled. Some people might be let in and others left outside to watch and hear but not take part. Who decided? And there you have it, wealth, organisation and power – the birth of bosses. Before you know it, you end up working for them. Such power might be maintained through sharper sticks or greater numbers but, before long, you have an aristocracy. They tell you how hard they worked to get where they are, or that their skills give them a unique perspec-

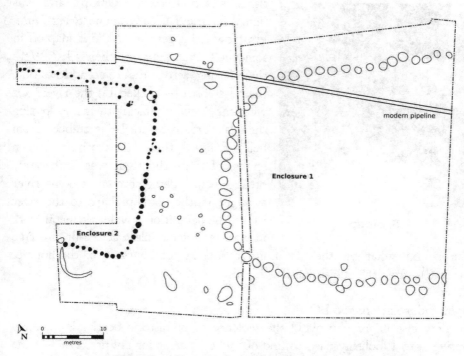

modern pipeline

Enclosure 1

Enclosure 2

N
0   10
metres

The start of bosses: the Bannockburn Cursuses

tive. But you're too tired to complain because you've been in a field all day and you're hungry, as there's not enough food because the bosses need to be paid... ho hum.

Evidence for Stirling's first murder?

Over time, as society became more complex, there was more to spend your wealth on and obviously more to accumulate. Another innovation brought by migrants was metal working, and at first this was just used to produce lots of bright shiny things. However, around 1,000 BC, the weather got colder and damper. Farms failed, stores ran out, and there was wave after wave of econom-ic migration. Inevitably, big people with big egos come up with a radical solu-tion – i.e. simply take what someone else has, preferably at spear or sword point. Those on the other side reasonably objected to their wee bit hill and glen becoming someone else's manifest destiny. They started to build walls and ram-parts and got their own weapons. This wee bit of bronze is the tip of a 3,000 year broken spear tip (which I held when it was still wet) recovered in the Forth at Cambuskenneth via metal detection by my good friends SARG (Scot-

Spear tip

tish Artefact Recovery Group), and was filmed for the TV programme *River Hunt-ers*. How did it get there? Did it snap off in someone's back between their ribs? Were they fleeing across the river at low tide, their last breaths choked by the river? Or were they defiantly facing their foe, spitting their last breath before being stabbed from hell's heart? I think the truth is no less strange. I think the spear was deliberately broken, before being thrown into the river as a gift to the gods, perhaps to the river itself. The deposition of valuable metal work in water is commonplace across Bronze Age Europe, but what was the gift meant to buy? A good harvest, or the hope of protection from the bullies and the thieves?

Splendid isolation: 500 BC

So how else might you avoid the violence of prehistoric Scotland? Well, in Spring 2019 I foolishly tried to find out when I went for my first swim of the year in the wonderful Loch Lubnaig[3] (258572, 710657; 56° 16′ 02″ N 4° 17′ 07″ W). As might be expected, the water was absolutely freezing and I swore quite profusely. But, dear reader, I was suffering on your behalf because I went to see the Loch Lubnaig Crannog, which comprises a big pile of stones in the middle of the loch with a warning flag on it. The mound measures 25m by 15m, and was discovered in 1968.

A real fixer-upper: the Loch Lubnaig crannog

Crannogs are artificial islands found across Scotland and Ireland. They combine stone and timber and there is a reconstruction of one, a timber roundhouse on stilts, in Loch Tay which is well worth a visit. There are several crannogs around Stirling, with a notable cluster in the Lake of Menteith. They have a wide date

---

3   Please be careful if you are not an experienced cold water swimmer!

range from the Bronze Age to the medieval period – but most of them date to the Iron Age.

As to why someone would want to live on an island, there are a range of options: you are generally safe on an artificial island in the middle of a loch (from both raiders and midges), but of course your crops and livestock can be stolen or burnt, in which case you will probably die over the winter. Hmm... not too sure that it's such a good idea. Another possibility is that the good farming ground was so restricted that houses moved to the loch to free up land. Yet another theory is that such settlements may be connected to harvesting a seasonal resource – perhaps salmon. Though why not simply put nets in the river? Regardless, having swam there, I would not fancy living there all year round. Though perhaps that itself was the point: it's really hard to live there, so if you do you must be very important. Whatever the reason, ultimately, the view is incredible as I'm sure you'll agree.

Cowie: a very, very, important place: 3000 BC to AD 200

By this point in the book, I'm sure you've gotten the basic single factor that influenced and controlled everything else after the Mesolithic. What? No? Okay, I'll tell you: cultivatable land. It was everything until around 1950. Yes, other things were important: mineral resources, river crossings, ports and so on. But if you had fertile land, you had people. With a population you could feed an army, and with an army you could challenge for power – whether you were on Islay or Shetland, or in Dunbar or Cowie. This was certainly how Bonnie Prince Charlie could raise an army that shook the British state to its core, from now-barren and empty hills and glens. Industrialisation of food production, consumerism and ambition drove, and continues to drive, people from rural locations even to this day.[4]

Have you ever been to Cowie? Most people seem to bypass it, but 4,000 years ago it was one of the most important places in Stirlingshire. The name Cowie is first recorded in the 12th century, and is likely to be Gaelic for wood. The village sits on high, dry, fertile ground projecting into the lost sea that once surrounded Stirling. So it had easily tillable ground and was surrounded by fish, shellfish and seaweed, all very tasty, healthy and free. All of which meant Cowie was a focus for our earliest ancestors. In fact, Cowie is home to Stirling's old-

---

[4] There is still net migration across Scotland. People move for jobs and opportunity and the bright lights of the cities. Equally, there is still migration of our best and brightest to London and all over the world and we miss all of you, do come back soon!

est houses, dating to between 5900-5610 BC, all of which are now under a wee housing estate on the north-western side of the village. The names of the streets reflect this ancient past: Roundhouse, Flint Crescent and Ochre Crescent (283591, 689563;56° 05′ 05″ N 3° 52′ 20″ W).

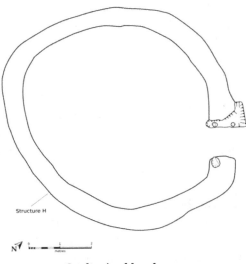

Structure H

N

Stirling's oldest house

Cowie was still important during the Celtic Iron Age, when it had its own hillfort and Stirling's only souterrain (both now quarried away). Souterrains are underground storage chambers probably used to accumulate agricultural surplus (though there is a lot of debate), which in Cowie's case was traded with the ever-hungry Roman Empire.

But Cowie was not just wealthy; it was special, and may even have been holy and sacred. This is certainly hinted at by its concentrations of cup and ring marked stones – one of the largest such concentrations in Central Scotland. These markings, beautiful and mysterious clusters and circles, are the earliest public art in the area. There are two main clusters (Castleton Wood and Fox-head Farm (285540, 688152; 56° 04′ 21″ N 3° 50′ 25″ W)), and they are quite tricky to find, but take your time and focus on outcrops of bedrock. You also have to walk in from Cowie, but it's a very pleasant walk with some amazing views back to the Castle and towards the Ochils. All of the stones are on private land and protected by law, so please respect them and leave gates as you find them.

The stone markings comprise a series of circles that look like ripples in a pond caused by thrown stones. We really don't know why they were carved, but they always seem to be in prominent locations with vast vistas in front of them. There is a lot of de-

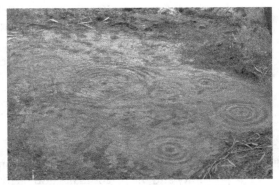

Cowie's amazing cup and ring marked stones

bate over their construction. Personally, I think they were probably constructed over decades by small family groups returning to the same spot, each generation adding to the long line of tradition: a place of worship, pilgrimage and perhaps healing. And for us, a place to breathe deep and connect with our shared past.

Chapter Two

The Start of History: AD 70-410

Roman Around Stirling

Slowly but surely, things got easier. New technologies arrived, including iron which made ploughing easier so more land could be farmed and generate more profit for the bosses. However, iron also made better and sharper weapons, so you had to build bigger and better forts. An absolutely incredible innovation though was the rotary quern. Now, you needed a quern – a stone mill for grinding grain by hand – to make flour, with which to make bread. Traditionally this had been done with a saddle quern, which you pushed and pulled backwards and forwards – very hard, back-breaking, monotonous work.[5] The rotary quern, however, required a much easier and fluid motion, just moving in a big circle. It freed up hundreds if not thousands of hours for people to do other things, and to generate more wealth. This might explain the presence of the Blair Drummond golden torcs (Google them) which appear to have been made in the Mediterranean and brought

A technological revolution

---

[5] Get a stone the size of a bag of sugar and push and pull it backwards and forwards over a paving slab for five hours, before you've eaten. See what I mean?

across Europe to end up in a hole next to the Teith around 200 BC.

The burying and hoarding of metalwork was commonplace in the last few centuries BC, and the pattern and nature of the material deposited suggests a society based on a series of small scale hierarchies, sometimes called Farmer Republics. These would be like small valley-based clans, who sometimes fight and sometimes collaborate with their nearest neighbours – who are likely to be cousins and second cousins[6] – but they're always rivals in some sense.

Now like any early adopters, these chiefs began to get wind of extremely fancy foreign goods from the Romans. Pottery, wine and fancy metalwork began to travel north, brought by traders, who in turn told stories of misty islands full of treasure back in Rome.[7] Though the truth was always disappointing – and in turn, Julius Caesar thought Britain was worth invading because of the vast quantities of fresh water pearls, and wound up disappointed that there was no gold or silver. However, the Romans slowly but surely moved north, hitting what became Scotland around AD 70-80. As to why they invaded, this is just what empires do: they stretch, they flex, and the only safe boundary is the coast – there was always a 'threat' over the horizon. Generals and emperors needed glory and wars were expensive, so it was not unreasonable to get those who benefitted from Rome's civilising presence to pay for the privilege. In time these newly conquered people would become citizens and pay taxes, but first they would become consumers. It was an attractive and recognisable pitch: "*You're not a barbarian are you, sir? Only barbarians drink the local beer; you ought to be drinking this expensive imported wine, surely? Good, I'm glad you see sense... now as you're drinking wine, you'll need a wine cup and a strainer. Oh no, you certainly can't drink this exclusive divine libation from a mere beaker. Now, with your wine, you'll need to eat the best stuff. I'm afraid bowls and spoons are no good; you need a plate and fork for olives and lark tongues to do it properly, and of course different courses need a range of sizes of fork...*"

---

6   *Asterix the Gaul* is a very good model.

7   Some will tell you a very early export from Scotland to Rome was Pontius Pilate, the man who condemned Christ to crucifixion. According to local legend he was born in Fortingall, Perthshire, next to the ancient yew, as a result of his father's liaison with a Caledonian woman on a very early diplomatic mission (of course, both father and son must have travelled via Stirling). Supporting evidence for this comes in the form of the discovery of a grave slab with P.P. on it – the current whereabouts of which are unknown. Now I'm all for a good story, but really!

Now, having created a desire, the Romans would supply one community but not another – divide and conquer. Anyway, the Romans made short work of the opposition and then gave us the most remarkable of gifts. Can you guess what it was? Here's a clue – did you travel today? Did you cycle, walk or drive, and could you get parked? It was pretty easy, wasn't it? The surface was firm, it would've been lit, there were street names and signs, and you didn't have to wait for the tide to go out to cross a river. Roads and bridges are absolutely central to every aspect of modern life; without them, everything would stop. The supply lines would stop first... Remember the early stages of the COVID-19 lockdown, how food and toilet paper vanished after a few days? In the past everything took longer, most things had to be sourced locally, and people died before medical attention could be summoned.

The gift was of course the road network which, ultimately, linked Stirling to Rome. People and ideas flowed along it: it bought Christianity and Pictish raiders from Inverness, who charged through Stirling and left a trail of destruction as far as Norfolk in AD 367. The same road was the main way into Stirling until the 1770s. Of course, this means it was used by everyone who ever travelled north or south of the city, from Edward II as he was preparing to meet Bruce and his destiny at the Battle of Bannockburn to Bonnie Prince Charlie.

The Road to Rome

Boom and Bust... Celtic Entrepreneurs or Quislings?: AD 100 to 140

The Romans secured their new territory with a line of forts and signal towers from Doune to the Tay (The Gask Ridge), to prepare for a push north that never came. After around 10-20 years or so they retreated to the line of what would become Hadrian's Wall – the troops were needed on the Danube. Some 50 years later, around AD 140, the Emperor Antonine needed a victory and so pushed north and built the Antonine Wall to secure his new lands, though this was abandoned roughly 20 years after it was started.

Over time, this coming and going across the Forth had quite an impact on Rome and its sense of self. Why on earth did Rome's mighty legions fail here, of all places in the known world? What exactly was different about Scotland? Those who had been on the front line knew all about how cold and wet Scotland was (shhh... don't tell Visit Scotland), the poor soils, the absence of big cities and the lack of gold. When this was reported to the imperial bean counters, everyone sensible concluded Scotland wasn't worth the effort... but no one told the poets and politicians. Caledonia (as Scotland was called) became shorthand for the edge of the world;[8] a mysterious, wild, unconquered place, full of dense impenetrable woods and marshes, populated by indomitable warriors. This led to a series of bloodcurdling proclamations about how horrible it was, and tales of 'mighty victories in Scotland'. One of my favourites is by Claudian, from the late 300s: '*What good is Britain's eternally harsh, cold climate and their uncharted seas? Orkney was drenched with Saxon slaughter; Shetland was warm with Pictish blood and icy Ireland wept for the heaps of Scottish dead*'. He did even better in the early 400s: '*The Legions came to guard the most remote Britons, who curbed the savage Scot and scanned the lifeless patterns tattooed on dying Picts*'. Now, it's worth pausing here to note that at this point Scots are from Ireland and 'Pict' means people north of Hadrian's Wall, which certainly includes raiders from north of Stirling but also might mean Geordies.[9]

But I have jumped ahead. The pinch point at Stirling across the Forth created opportunities for those who understood the ground, because it was the

---

[8] This has led some to get confused about precisely when we became Christian. Roman author Tertullian from Carthage suggested that by AD 200 all of Britain not conquered by Rome had become Christian – but this was just fake news... a bit like Donald Trump lying about how much bigger his Presidential inauguration was than Barack Obama's!

[9] For non-UK readers, Geordies are from Newcastle in England and a thoroughly nice bunch.

only way to move goods from north to south or vice versa. Now, depending on your view this might be described as supply and demand, taxation or a giant protection racket. Either way, someone charged you to 'facilitate' your crossing. Now let's be charitable, said someone may have maintained paths and bridges or kept down local bandits. However, whatever they did, they accumulated wealth and power from controlling the crossing.

Torwood Broch Stirling's oldest standing building

Now I know what you're thinking: how would you show off all this new found cash?[10] You couldn't buy a Porsche, or go on a cruise – though you could certainly get a new tattoo. If you still had something left over, the big fashion accessory at the time was... drumroll... a broch. Brochs are normally associated with northern Scotland, but there are a few in the south and most of these are around Stirling. Brochs are tower-like structures, with the best evidence for upper floors in prehistoric Europe. The biggest one in the area – and the oldest standing structure near Stirling by nearly a thousand years – is Torwood broch (283326, 685004; 56° 02′ 37″ N 3° 52′ 28″ W). It is very cool and contains the ar-

---

[10]   Just for clarity they didn't really have cash – there were no coins made by Scots for 1,000 years!

ea's oldest staircase, cupboard, and just maybe a shrine (a face down cup-marked stone in the staircase). Two thousand years ago brochs were exotic and hard to build: an absolutely, no-doubt-about-it, must-have status symbol.

Anyway, to return to the Romans and their Empire, the Gask Ridge was probably manned by 5,000-6,000 soldiers while the Antonine Wall had around 9,000 – and these guys were always hungry. Scottish farms were the closest suppliers, but this also fitted with the Romans' preferred approach. They wanted to encourage local businesses so that they could be taxed – I mean, you really can't tax an empty valley, can you? So both military occupations had an enormous impact on the local economy, and as a result more brochs and broch-like structures were built. Over the years I've worked on five of these structures. They are all slightly different, as people had differing amounts of money so they built varying designs. Ultimately they were all trying to do outdo their cousins up the road. Now, elaborate architecture wasn't just about showing off; it could also communicate a political message. Might brochs have suggested a non-Roman identity, perhaps a free past or the still free north? What went through the minds of the people who traded with the Romans, and how were they viewed by those that didn't? If, instead of the Romans (who most people like), you think of the Nazis and Vichy France, how does that change your view?

One of the people that traded with the Romans built an elaborate defended house in Stirling's King's Park (278146, 693079; 56° 06′ 54″ N 3° 57′ 41″ W) which I discovered in 2017. We did a big dig here in the summer of 2019, and again in 2020. Now the thing about archaeology is that it's a bit like love:

Stirling's oldest thumbprint

all about the small things. This wee object (you may have to squint to see it) is just bigger than my thumb nail, and yet it packs a big punch. It was found by Shelly Schermer, who came from the USA to our fair city to join us in the 2019 season. So what is it? Well, it's a bit of fired clay, a piece of daub from a wattle and daub screen (clay pressed into wicker work). You can just make out the thumbprint of one of your ancestors as they moulded the clay – this is Stirling's oldest finger print. The other side shows the impression of the clay around the wicker work. It demonstrates that the house was burnt down – but more about that later.

Now anyone who's met me knows my love of very bad jokes: poor, groan-inducing, Christmas cracker rejects. One of my favourites is: when is a door not a door? I can almost hear you scream – when it's ajar! However, in archaeology, a door is not a door when it's no longer there; when all that's left is the impressions caused by the repeated opening and closing of the door as it welcomed guests and was locked against intruders. The object in the picture is a pivot stone from the King's Park fort.

The oldest door in Stirling

We don't think doors had hinges at the time; they were secured to a pole, which was embedded in a rock, which was slowly ground down. We found three pivot stones on the site, indicating a process of ongoing maintenance of the structure and its door. Now, while this building was made of stone, it will have also used timber and thatch – all of which required regular renewal and slowly but surely will have filled up with vermin, ticks, fleas, lice and will have smelled rather ripe to say the least.

The doorway to this dark smelly space, marked by the pivot stone, welcomed Roman soldiers, who came to impose peace, to civilise this last wee corner of free Europe, to tell us how to live, and make us pay taxes for the new road that ran south all the way to Rome. But that is another, bigger, story.

What the Romans left after the destruction of Leckie Broch

Of course, the thing about dealing with an empire is that the soldiers follow orders, which can change at a whim: one minute they're trying to trade, and the next you're in the way. To make things worse, our King's Park fort-builder was likely viewed as a barbarian by the Romans and a traitor by those to the north – a very dangerous position to be in. On top of that, at least one of the brochs round Stirling (Leckie 269263, 694005; 56° 07' 15" N 4° 06' 16" W) had been destroyed in fire and flame by the Roman army (excavation recovered a Roman ballista bolt in its smouldering ruins). Might a similar fate have preserved that thumb print? In fact, some 70-80% of the excavated sites were destroyed by fire, including Mote Hill (279327, 694467; 56° 07' 39" N 3° 56' 35" W), which ended being burnt so intensely that it vitrified. This is an incredible process whereby a timber-laced rampart is burnt to such a high temperature that the stone melts and fuses. It would have glowed: a vivid, red hot statement of destructive power, the smoke visible across the valley all day long and the fire even further at night. But did the Romans really do it all? We certainly know from elsewhere in the Empire that the Romans could and did commit genocide, and would do it Scotland (see below).

The largest bit of vitrified stone in Stirling, from the Abbey Craig

Most of the excavated sites were filled with expensive Roman goods which were carefully dismantled before their destruction by fire (e.g. Fairy Knowe, Buchlyvie). Why would the Romans even bother to do such a thing? None of the sites date to after 200 AD; they all seem to end with the abandonment of the Antonine Wall. I think that when all this Roman wealth vanished as they retreated south, the entire economy of the Forth Valley crashed. Perhaps those too closely tied to the Romans fled south. What was the fate of all those children with Roman fathers?[11] This really was the collapse of an entire way of life. In the resulting chaos, I think most people fell back on older rituals and gods; the wealth and status created by trade with the Romans was in some way so tainted that it had to be disposed of. It was piled in the houses, which were then dismantled before the terrible beauty of a bonfire – a last celebration for a way of life changed utterly forever. So while we can be clear that the Romans destroyed some sites, it's also clear that the locals destroyed even more and that this was in some way a ritual response to the retreat of the Empire to the south.

The Final Frontier?: AD 200.

Where was the capital of the Roman Empire? I can almost hear you shout Rome or Constantinople. Well, yes and no. During the later Empire, as the emperor became more and more powerful, the functioning centre was wherever he was and people travelled from what is now Italy to petition him. Now, you remember I told you about Scotland's reputation in the Roman Empire? About how it was a wild, indomitable place, where men were men and heroes were made, but that it was really all just spin and hype?

---

[11]   Certainly not as much fun as *Life of Brian*.

Following Agricola, Hadrian and Antonine's failure to conquer Scotland, Emperor Septimius Severus thought he was big enough and ugly enough to sort it out himself. The local people, the Maeatae, had been causing trouble with the tribe to the north, the Caledonians, in breach of their treaty obligations. The Maeatae are Stirling's first recorded people, and their name survives in two local hills: Dumyat (Dun Maeatae: the fort of the Maeatae) and Myot Hill. Dumyat dominates Stirling's landscape, and in September 2019 I led its first archaeological excavation. We dug the outer ditches and recovered some charcoal and burnt bone – the remains of someone's dinner dating to between AD 437-631 AD.

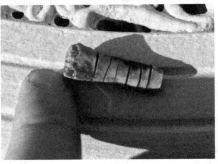

Roman author Cassius Dio describes the Maeatae, who '*inhabit wild and waterless mountains and desolate and swampy plains, and possess neither walls, cities, nor tilled fields, but live on their flocks, wild game, and certain*

The remains of a Maeatae's dinner

fruits; for they do not touch the fish which are there found in immense and inexhaustible quantities. They dwell in tents, naked and unshod, possess their women in common, and in common rear all the offspring. Their form of rule is democratic for the most part, and they are very fond of plundering; consequently they choose their boldest men as rulers. They go into battle in chariots, and have small, swift horses; there are also foot-soldiers, very swift in running and very firm in standing their ground. For arms they have a shield and a short spear, with a bronze apple attached to the end of the spear-shaft, so that when it is shaken it may clash and terrify the enemy; and they also have daggers. They can endure hunger and cold and any kind of hardship; for they plunge into the swamps and exist there for many days with only their heads above water, and in the forests they support themselves upon bark and roots, and for all emergencies they prepare a certain kind of food, the eating of a small portion of which, the size of a bean, prevents them from feeling either hunger or thirst.'

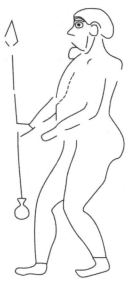

A Maeatae, or his Perthshire cousin?

I resisted the urge to make witty[12] but snide comments all the way through this nonsense. The majority is standard rhetoric about how wild, primitive and cold Scotland was, and how difficult it would be for Septimius to invade such a barbaric place. However, this is the first written description of Stirling and reflects the landscape before the peat was cleared. There are clearly some details drawn from life, those 'bronze apples' at the end of spears match weapons illustrated carved stones found just to the north of Stirling. And all that stuff about plunging into swamps and having nothing to eat is exactly how my daughters described our last camping holiday.

Anyway, a Scottish trip was exactly what Septimius wanted to toughen up his two sons, the future Emperors Geta and Antoninus. Cassius tells us they had been up to no good and '*outraged women and abused boys, they embezzled money, and made gladiators and charioteers their boon companions, emulating each other in the similarity of their deeds, but full of strife in their rivalries; for if the one attached himself to a certain faction, the other would be sure to choose the opposite side. And at last they were pitted against each other in some kind of contest with teams of ponies and drove with such fierce rivalry that Antoninus fell out of his two-wheeled chariot and broke his leg*'. All of which sounds like a typical Bullingdon Club bash – not that I'd know though.

So around 208, Septimius brought his family to Britain, and a year later he invaded Scotland with his wife and oldest son Antoninus who, for reasons that will become clear, he did not entirely trust. Across the Empire, the Romans campaigned in the same way: after a day's march they built a temporary camp, all to the same design and all of which contained hundreds of bread ovens[13] (it transpires that the Romans cooked bread like we cook pizza – they built a fire over some stones, under a soil

Scotland's oldest pizza oven

---

[12]   Editor to Murray: Really? You think this stuff is witty?

[13]   The bread oven illustrated is from my excavations at Kintore.

and wicker work dome, and when it was hot enough they pushed the embers to the side and cooked on the hot stones!) The camp also contained hundreds of tents, latrine pits and so on (they got very, very smelly). The one exception to the general marching camp construction across the entire Roman Empire were the camps built for Septimius, like the one at Craigarnhall (275837, 698179;56° 09′ 36″ N 4° 00′ 03″ W) near Bridge of Allan, all of which have a wee annex to the side. This is where we think the Emperor and his family stayed and which, therefore, for a few days around June 209 was the capitol of the Roman Empire.

Septimius Severus conducted a particularly savage invasion of Scotland and, as Cassius famously quotes, he demanded that '...*no one escape sheer destruction, no one our hands, not even the babe in the womb of the mother, if it be male; let it nevertheless not escape sheer destruction.*' However, it's not precisely certain that this did happen, or whether or not it's merely spin!

Septimius will have stayed at Craigarnhall on his way back from this murderous campaign, but this time he will have had captives, presumably including the tartan trew-wearing Caledonian who we heard about earlier. This poor soul will likely have been captured around Perth and may even have been the local chieftain Argentocoxos, or someone related to him, with whom Severus had concluded a treaty but which he later broke. He was most likely destined for death in the Colosseum as a celebration of the great Roman victory. Can you imagine his confusion and terror? The weeks of travel, the sight of Rome, buildings of stone, and then the baying crowds — were there lions and tigers?

Ultimately the campaign proved very difficult for Severus, not because of the killing — that was standard Roman policy — but due to the fact that he was dying and Antoninus was plotting to kill both him and Geta. Severus died in York in 211, and his two children raced back to Rome to secure their thrones. When they got back, Antonius ordered Geta's assassination — it was successful, and Geta died in his mother's arms.

Antoninus then changed his name to Caracella, one of history's blackest tyrants, and ordered the systematic *damnatio memoriae* of his brother.[14] Geta's face was removed from all paintings, coins were melted down, statues smashed, his name erased from all records, and it became a capital offence to speak or write Geta's name. It's estimated that around 20,000 of Geta's friends, advisers and supporters were massacred and, in amongst all the bloodshed, Caracalla forgot all about Scotland, which went all quiet for the next 80 years. Now, why this happened is unclear, and it may be because Severus's slaughter really hap-

---

[14]   A trick Stalin later perfected.

pened. Certainly, there are no known new settlements in Scotland between 200 and 300 AD, it really was as if there had been a massive genocide.

From '*Hitherto semi-naked Picts*'... to *Kings and Priests*: AD 287 to 700
Slowly but surely, life returned to Scotland. Rome was still there, a lumbering giant, an ageing superpower, full of unimaginable wealth and an obvious target for raiding. The Roman writer Eumenius first referred to the aggressive anti-Roman people north of Hadrian's Wall in 297 as Picti (Picts). Picti was a derogatory ethnic slur, probably referencing local tattooing – i.e. 'painted people', or perhaps more like *painted pygmies*, designed to insult, degrade and 'other'. Gradually, 'Pict' began to be associated with people from what would become Scotland. Just to stress this point: Pict was a term coined by the Romans and was not what the inhabitants of Scotland called themselves. Throughout the 300s there were a series of back and forth raids between Picts and the Roman Empire. Emperor Constantius Chlorus[15] invaded around 306, but the Pictish raids gained ever greater force, penetrating deeper and deeper into the Empire. Eventually in 367, in a series of apparently coordinated incursions, the Saxons along with two Pictish tribes (the Verturiones from around Inverness and the Dicalydones from Perthshire) and the Irish Attacotti captured and killed Roman officials. Emperor Theodosius eventually chased them away but still the raids continued until eventually Stilicho, who has been described as the last of the Roman Generals, invaded and defeated the Picts. But it was not enough and in 410, after over one hundred years of unwinnable conflict, the Romans abandoned Britain... the bean counters had won.

The subsequent collapse of Roman civilisation is described by Gildas, an angry 6th century monk born in Romanised Scotland, 200 years later. He viewed the whole thing as God's divine punishment on what had become a decadent and immoral society. And he really, really didn't like the Picts:

"*...the terrible hordes of Scots and Picts... when the sun is high and the heat increasing, dark swarms of worms emerge from the narrow crevices of their holes. Differing partly in their habits, yet alike in one and the same thirst for bloodshed – in a preference also for covering their villainous faces with hair rather than their nakedness of body with decent clothing... [their] barbed weapons... are not idle: by them the wretched citizens are dragged from the walls and dashed to the ground.*"

---

[15]   Constantius was the father of Constantine the Great – the emperor who made Christianity the official religion of the Roman Empire.

Ouch.

Between 450 and 496, Saint Patrick wrote a letter to the King of Dumbarton Rock, Coroticus, who may have held power over Stirling, complaining that the King had captured and enslaved free-born Christians and sold them to the 'abominable, wicked, and apostate Picts'. It's not clear if this refers to a Pictish Kingdom, or simply a more general insult. However, the use of a Roman insult would have lent authority and gravitas to St Patrick. Certainly, I'd argue that the reference to 'apostate' – someone who recants their Christianity – underlines the insulting nature of the words, as the Old Testament makes clear: apostasy is punishable by death.

By the late 600s St Adomnan, an Abbot of Iona and biographer of Columba, was in no doubt that the Picts were a people; there were Pictish priests in Ireland (Iogenan) and kings in Scotland (Bruide son of Derile). Bruide signed up to Adomnan's Law of the Innocents, a remarkable treaty protecting non-combatants during conflict. This treaty is especially interesting as it's full of details details about how rubbish life for women was. One section describes the many ways in which a woman should not die, implying that such atrocities were commonplace: 'that women be not in any manner killed by men, through slaughter or any other death, either by poison, or in water, or in fire, or by any other beast, or in a pit, or by dogs, but that they shall die in their lawful bed'.

The slightly later writer Bede, from Northumbria, also thought that the Picts were a people. By around 900 Pictland had become Alba, with a distinctly Irish Gaelic identity.

This of course raises two questions: how did a Roman ethnic slur become a symbol of political unity and pride and how did it get replaced by a focus on Irish origins? In answer to the first question, presumably later, literate people tried to find references to themselves in Roman history and came across accounts of Picts. They then said 'Oh, that must be us. What do you think?', 'Definitely us – wow, aren't we impressive? We beat the Romans! We absolutely rock! C'mon the Picts...' This is the birth of Scottish exceptionalism, and it gets echoed in any number of not-bad Victorian poems. For example: Alexander Stewart's The Battlefields of Stirling, which links the victories of both Wallace and Bruce to the defeat of the legions:

> Long ages past, on Carron's shore[16]
> With iron front they stood,

---

[16]   The River Carron lies just to the north of the Antonine Wall.

And Rome's proud eagles backwards bore, –
Their plumage stained with blood.

But you'll have to wait for an explanation of the later Picitsh rebranding to Alba.

Chapter Three

The Dark Ages:
AD 400-700

Rage, Rage Against the Dying of the Light

Academics (and I suppose I have to include myself in this bracket) don't talk about the Dark Ages any more. The term had long been used to describe the time of the destruction of literate Christian societies by a series of illiterate, pagan raiders and described by Gildas. It is the source of the Arthurian myth cycle, i.e. a Christian warrior fighting in the old Roman style against barbarians – he wins some battles, there's a brief glorious renaissance of peace and stability before the horde overwhelms everything.[17] Academics now talk about this time as the Early Medieval Period and processes of elite adaption and social change... while this is not quite as much fun, it is absolutely more accurate: 'Dark Age' is ultimately misleading and incorrect.

After the collapse of the Romanised order, society broke into smaller units, all of whom were at war with each other – hence the need for Adomnan's *Law of the Innocents*. Scotland became divided into four main blocks: Picts north of the Forth, Angles to the South-East, Dalriadan[18] Scots (who, of course, were Irish) and the Britons to the west and in the middle. None of this is to do with genetics; it's all politics. The Britons, unlike the Picts, had in some way associated themselves with the Romans, becoming Christian and drawing

---

17   Is that also not the plot of most zombie films?

18   Academics now prefer to use Dál Riata, but as this is a general book I've kept to the older form.

authority from perceived Roman origins. There were at least four British King-doms in southern Scotland: Manau around Stirling, the Gododdin in East Lo-thian, Alt Clywd around Dumbarton Rock and Rheged to the south-west. The Angles expanded and took over Gododdin and then eventually fought for Ma-nau and Rheged. The collapse of Alt Clywd led to another kingdom called Strathclyde.

But before all that, I have to talk about the Picts again. We heard earlier how the term 'Pict' moved from being an insult to a self-adopted symbol of power and pride. Archaeologists also use the term as a shorthand for both a period and class of objects – the Pictish Period and Pictish symbol stones. What we call Pictish symbol stones are part of a wider movement of late to middle 1st millennium AD insular art. This art is most often associated with carved stones and mostly occurs in the area that came to be dominated by the people who called themselves the Picts in the Pictish Period.

The first people to self-identify as Picts, those who read about themselves in Roman texts, lived around Inverness in a kingdom known as Fortiu. They expanded south and north, carving out an empire. This Pictish Empire eventual-ly conquered Stirling, which was at the core of Manau. There are, however, no Pictish symbol stones in Stirling, although there are definitely Pictish Period carved stones (as we'll find out). So Pictish symbol stones were carved and created both before and after the core of the Pictish Period by various peoples, not all of whom claimed to be Picts at first but most of whom ended up being conquered at some point by them. It is this that Adomnan and Bede were writing about. Equally, this Pictish kingdom was likely to have been a short-lived political identity to help bind all these newly conquered peoples and places. Phew... don't worry, there's no exam at the end.

The Clack of Manau. Please note it's the wee stone on top and not the big pillar (291104, 691885; 56° 06′ 26″ N 3° 45′ 09″ W)

Back to Stirling which, as we've heard, was in Manau and populated by the Miathi, the likely descendants of the Maeatae. Manau contains *man- or *mon-, meaning either projecting or high land, and probably refers to The Ochils. The name survives in four different place names: Clackmannan (The Stone of Manau); Slamannan (The Plain of Manau); Rathmannan (The fort of Manau) and Cromennane in Balfron (The boundary of Manau). All of these names seem to mark the boundaries of Manau, meaning it stretched from Balfron to Fife. The jewel in its crown was the strategic crossing of the Forth at Stirling. But what does the name Stirling actually mean? Before we go, on there is no connection to sterling, the name for British currency; this is a myth from the 15th century spread by a Dundonian historian of dubious reputation called Hector Boece.

The first recorded version, '*Striuelin*', dates from around 1124 when the burgh was established by David I. This appears to be a corrupted version of the Gaelic '*srib-linn*' ('stream pool'), although the modern Gaelic rendering is '*Sruighlea*'. The name derives from the place at which the River Forth became tidal, or perhaps better, where the uppermost reach of the Forth estuary became navigable, possibly reflecting an early harbour here. Of course this means that Stirling was not the name of the settlement, although quite what it *was* called is unknown.

At this time literacy was generally a Christian thing and so, as you might expect, all of the earliest references to Stirling are connected to Saints. So there is a reference to a nunnery founded by the Irish St Monenna around 500, while 50 years later St Cadoc – with the help of a resurrected, formerly evil, giant called Caw who was subsequently reformed[19] – built a monastery here and spent seven years in the area. Around the same time, St Serf (the foster father of St Kentigern, the Patron Saint of Glasgow) was performing miracles around what is now Stirling University (where, during exams, prayers for miracles are still heard to this day) and St Kessog was active to the west of Stirling. Other saints are of course available.

These early Christians performed a variety of roles from conversions to the ministry of existing communities who had converted during the Roman Empire. The role of these early missionaries ended up being downplayed by the success of the Columban Mission as narrated by Adomnan – it is this story most people have heard. Around the 570s, St Columba travelled to Inverness and had a magical duel with a druid before converting the local Pictish king.

---

[19]   Honestly, I'm not making this stuff up... though perhaps someone else was!

Bede credits Columba with converting the northern Picts, while the southern Picts were converted earlier by St Ninian. In both cases the central roles of Ninian and Columba was overplayed and the truth was more likely to have been a slow, gradual process of centuries of brave, individual acts of faith. However, gradually, other Scottish church traditions began to reassert themselves, as we shall see.

Returning to Stirling, very little survives of these churches beyond the odd name. There is Kilmadock (*Church of the Beloved Cadoc*) (270642, 702483; 56° 11' 50" N 4° 05' 11" W), which is also associated with Eggles and Annet (these are are found in the slightly wider area), the only example in Scotland. Eggles and Annet are not some rubbish 70s comedy act, but Gaelic names for ancient churches: Eggles derives from the latin Ecclesia and Annet is 'old church'. This presumably reflects the importance of what Cadoc and Caw established. However, it is always possible it was rededicated to Cadoc later on. There is another Eggles in Stirling (now St Ninians) and there was one at Falkirk (it was originally Egglesbrecht: the speckled church).

In addition, there are odd fragments of carved stones. There are a few at St Ninians and, until very recently, almost nothing at all at Old Kilmadock. There had been a stone with writing on it at Kilmadock which was discovered around 1900 and promptly vanished. Now, I can just hear you ask, where did it vanish to? Well, I am indebted to my friend Peter Herbert who discovered the stone in Oxford's Ashmolean Museum where it rejoices in the accession number

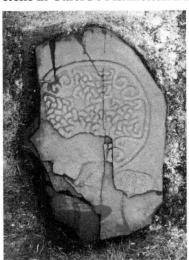 

Recent discoveries by the wonderful ROOK: an inscribed cross-slab and a bear/wolf figure

AN1966.1175. Now quite how it got there is unknown, and certainly its expropriation from Kilmadock would be against the law today, but it was a different age.

Peter and Pat Herbert are active founding members of ROOK (Rescuers of Old Kilmadock) who, along with Ro and Allan Drowley, are helping to conserve this ancient place. In 2019 they found two carved stones: a fragment of bear or wolf, and an inscribed cross which seems to date to between 500 to 700. Similar crosses have been found in Angus and Aberdeen, and are associated with Irish missionaries from Iona. Certainly we can see evidence of their route through the dedications to Ionian Saints: Columba (Inchmahome) and Adomnan (Fintry). This of course raises the question as to the presence of Irish missionaries at a site dedicated to a Welsh Saint. The most likely answer is simply that all of these traditions were merging and feeding on each other; there was fluidity and variation. The same thing happened in the very early church: St Paul's letter to the Galatians deals with the issue of whether or not newly converting Christians need to become Jews before becoming Christian, i.e. whether Christians should be circumcised. Given that circumcision tends to happen to young boys and at this point most conversions were of adults, I'm pleased to confirm that Paul didn't think they needed to have anything sliced off.

A smaller controversy followed when the Catholic Church tried to convert the Angles from the south. You will remember that following the collapse of Roman society, Christianity was almost extinguished and only survived on the fringes: Scotland, Ireland and Wales. Well, in 575 a monk named Gregory spotted some English Christian slaves[20] in Rome. When he became Pope he sent his pal Augustine to help and, in 596, he started to convert England. The Kingdom of Northumbria was on quite friendly terms with the Columban church but it was clear that there were some differences between Iona and Rome, so in 664 at Whitby a synod was organised to decide which tradition Northumbria would follow. The differences were rather small,[21] including the calculation of

---

[20]   Between Patrick and Gregory there is quite a lot about the horror of Christians being enslaved – just remember this when we come to the 12th century!

[21]   Just to be clear, there really was no independent 'Celtic' Church. Yes, it was slightly different, but it wasn't a big theological deal; rather a question of church politics. It certainly wasn't anything like the differences created by the Reformation!

Easter and different haircuts. The decision was taken to follow the Catholic[22] model. This was on the basis that while St Columba was a holy man, it was just that the Catholic Church was founded by St Peter, who was closer to Christ. (I mean, he was an apostle, right? So he must be on better terms?) This marked the beginning of the end of Columban authority and in 717 meant that the Ionian church had been expelled from Pictland.[23]

But we are definitely jumping ahead. These lost and conquered kingdoms became associated with a golden British past, the key stories of which survive in medieval Welsh poetry where the land is known as *Yr Hen Ogledd*: the Old North[24]. The most famous of these poems is the *Gododdin*, which features the first mention of King Arthur. These poems also reveal a series of royal genealogies with Roman origins: the Kings of Rheged claimed descent from a 4th century Roman General, Magnus Maximus. The eighth and ninth kings of Gwynedd claimed descent from a ruler of Manau called Cunedda, who in turn claimed descent from Padarn Beisrudd ap Tegid (Paternus of the Red Cloak[25]) which may imply some form of Roman official. The kings of Strathclyde count Cinhill and Cluim among their ancestors, which might be Quintilius and Clemens, classic Roman names.

---

[22]   Not for nothing does 'catholic' mean all-encompassing!

[23]   However, while the Northumbrians rejected the Columban church they do appear to have adopted Pictish tattooing. A Papal legate, Bishop George of Ostia, complained in 787 about people adopting such a heathen, superstitious practice. To date, despite the best efforts of the greatest minds in Scottish archaeology, no evidence for any Pictish tattoo parlours has ever been recovered, though the search continues.

[24]   Yes, an ancestral version of Welsh was once spoken around Stirling before being replaced by an earlier version of Irish around 900 (Menstrie and Dollar are both 'Welsh' words in origin). The difference is best expressed through Aber- and Inver-; both mean mouth of a river, but Aber is Welsh or P-Gaelic, and Inver is Irish or Q-Gaelic.

[25]   The cloak was one of the thirteen treasures of Britain and would perfectly fit any hero – but not a coward. Other treasures included rings, cloaks of invisibility, magical chariots and swords. But perhaps the worst of the treasures was The Knife of Llawfrodedd the Horseman, which allowed 24 men to eat at once. I mean, really; he must have been at the end of the line when the treasures were handed out.

The poems are dominated by accounts of raids and battles by brave and heroic kings, and in a poem called *The War Band's Return* Urien of Rheged is praised for raiding Manau (quite a distance from Galloway to Stirling) and recovering:

> *In one year*
> *One that provides*
> *Wine and bounty and mead,*
> *And manliness without enmity,*
> *And a musician excelling,*
> *With a swarm of spears about him.*
> *With ribbons at their heads,*
> *And their fair appearances.*
> *Every one went from his presence,*
> *They came into the conflict,*
> *And his horse under him.*
> *Purposing the affair of Manau.*
> *And more harmony,*
> *Advantage flowing about his hand.*
> *Eight score[26] of one colour*
> *Of calves and cows.*
> *Milch cows and oxen.*
> *And every fair need.*

These raids were exactly like those undertaken by the Maeatae and the Verturiones against the southern Roman provinces. They provided treasures to be spread amongst followers, binding them in pursuit of glory but also supporting the local economies. The same Urien who raided Manau is praised for his generosity ('*as you gather in, so you give away*'), and is called '*a battle winning lord, cattle-raider*'. But there was a terrible price to be paid. *The Battle of Gwen Ystrad* describes a clash between Rheged and people from Yorkshire, and features mounds of dead bodies, bloody clothes and battle-scarred flesh.

In amongst these raids were genuine invasions; people were killed, territory shifted and Manau was slowly but surely carved up. The first indication of a loss is connected with our friend Pardarn, from Manau, and his magical cloak. This implies that some portion of Manau, if not all of it, had been conquered by the Gododdin (the people of the eponymous people) quite early on, perhaps around 400-500. Adomnan relates a battle between Dalriada and the Miathi at

---

[26]   Eight score is 120.

Circinn, which is possibly in Manau, around 594. During the battle the Dalriadan King Aedan mac Gabrain won but lost two of his sons, Arthur[27] and Echoid Find. This is the last time that the Miathi are mentioned and we assume that Manau was from then on under Dalriadan control.

However, this presumed control of Manau did not go unchallenged, and in 643 Eugein of Dumbarton Rock defeated Dalriadan Domnall Brecc (grandson of Aedan mac Gabrain) at the Battle of Strathcarron on the southern fringes of Manau, probably around the Carron Valley Reservoir. This clash is described in a small stanza *The Strath Caruin Awdl* which concludes with '*and crows picked at the head of Domnall Brecc*'.[28]

Where Domnall Breck Fell, in the shadow of Meikle Bin

From the middle of the 6th century, East Lothian's Gododdin had been raided by the Anglian Kingdom of Bernicia for at least a generation, and a terrible battle between them is the key element of their eponymous poem. The siege of Edinburgh in 638 probably reflects the final stages of their conquest of the Gododdin. Between 642 and 654 the main force from Northumbria was led by Oswy, who oversaw the Synod of Whitby where Columba was assessed and found wanting. Oswy came under pressure from another English king to the south, Penda of Mercia, and in 655 was pushed all the way to Urbs Iudeu (or Guidi). Now, there is a lot of debate about precisely where Iudeu was. Certainly the Forth was known as The Sea of Iudeu and the options for where Iudeu was include Blackness, Stirling or somewhere in Fife. What it does show is the degree of English penetration into what

---

[27]   The first recorded real person in Scotland to be called Arthur!

[28]   This of course brings to mind the traditional and very gruesome Medieval Border ballad 'Twa Corbies', which was also written during a period of prolonged raiding. The poem describes two crows discussing where to eat that evening, and one suggests the corpse of a new slain knight:

Ye'll sit on his white hause-bane,
And I'll pike out his bonny blue een;
Wi ae lock o his gowden hair
We'll, theek our nest when it grows bare.

is now Scotland. Certainly by 681AD, Northumbrian King Ecgfrith was so confident that Manau was secure that he established a bishopric at Abercorn for Bishop Trumwine.

This secure base seems to have prompted the Angles to penetrate deep into Pictland, which unfortunately ended in disaster at the Battle of Nechtansmere (somewhere around Inverness), which was won by the Pictish King of Fortriu.[29] This was such a major victory that Trumwine fled as fast as he could to Whitby, over 200 miles away. This, however, was not the end of the Anglian threat and in 711 an English army slaughtered a Pictish one on the Plain of Manau, which lay between the Carron and the Avon. Within a generation though, Picts had completely taken over Manau and imposed their own institutions: land division, establishment of churches and legal offices - all of which are the most southern examples of their type at the time in Scotland. Pictish land divisions are called 'davochs' and the ones in Clackmannanshire are all close to Tillicoultry. The village of Coalsnaughtan appears to preserve the name of Pictish King Nechtan. Another Pictish administrative addition was 'thanes',[30] officers appointed by the King and there were only two of them south of the Forth, one in Manau (at Falkirk) and one in Haddington. Finally, the Picts also estab-

Pictish religious imperialism: Logie Kirk

---

[29]   Fortriu is the ancestor kingdom descended from the Verturiones who were involved in the 367 Barbarian Conspiracy.

[30]   While 'thane' is clearly an English word, it's likely to be a translation of an older Pictish position: 'taoiseach', which survives in Gaelic as 'leader' – the Irish equivalent of the UK Prime Minister is the Taoiseach.

• • •

lished a church at Logie[31] to the north of Stirling. In this context '*logie*' is likely to be derived from the Latin locus meaning place and in this context '*holy place*' (281527, 696977; 56° 09′ 03″ N 3° 54′ 31″ W).

---

[31]   I hope you'll forgive me, but I've put two images of the kirk, before and after its restoration by the wonderful Logie Old Graveyard Group, of which I am the chair now that the hard work has been done, all of which was coordinated by the wonderful Joe and Eleanor Young.

Chapter Four

From Picts to Scots: AD 700-1000

Don't Forget the Vikings

At some point around 900 Pictland was rebranded as Alba,[32] and Picts became Scots for contemporary political reasons.[33] This was linked to Kenneth MacAl-pin, ostensibly the first King of Scotland, who is supposed to have beaten the Picts around Cambuskenneth Abbey in 834 and to have unified Pictland with Dalriada in 843.[34] After this, Pictish laws were overturned and some older

---

[32]   One of the traditions of medieval Europe was that people were assumed to have an eponymous founder. Albanus and Britos were the sons of Ela-nius, establishing Alba as an ancient and equal kingdom to Britos in what became Britain. However, this was later tweaked by Geoffrey of Mon-mouth in the 12th century to imply that Albanos was the son of Britos, which implies that Britos – and in this context England – was the senior and therefore dominant kingdom in Britain, a concept that Edward I glee-fully seized upon.

[33]   If anyone is in doubt that or why an elite group might change its name for political reasons, I refer you to the Saxe-Coburg-Gothas: Britain's Royal Family, who changed their name to Windsor during World War I as Ger-man things were unpopular. It might also be worth pointing out that their claim to the throne derived from their descent from the Stewarts!

[34]   An intriguing legacy of this union might be the office of Mormaer. Mormaers are argued to be native great officers of state, semi-

sources have argued that there was an ethnic cleansing of the Picts. The truth is more complex, and we certainly don't fully understand it. Kenneth was a member of the Pictish royal family, which had intermarried with the Dalriadan one for generations. It is likely that whatever happened took place around 900 and was projected back to Kenneth's time to give it legitimacy. This change also coincided with a shift in the kingdom's focus from Inverness to Tayside and Fife, with a capitol in Forteviot, when the focus of royal coronations became Scone. This new kingdom had a distinctly Dalriadan tone with the elite claiming Irish and Gaelic origins rather than Pictish.

Alba is likely to be similar to words in both Pictish and Gaelic for Britain (e.g. Albion), and may represent an attempt to create a new unified identity. As to why the new kingdom had more of a west coast identity, this may have come from an influx of refugees as the Vikings took over parts of Dalriada and, equally, the Pictish elite was impacted by fighting the Vikings. However, political allegiance and origins can and do 'change', and we can find more modern parallels with the twisting of the Medieval Scottish court between France and England.[35]

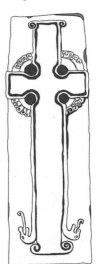 

A definitely *not* Pictish Stone

Nothing, however, changed the basic situation: the Picts and then the Scots continued to raid south of the Forth. Kenneth MacAlpin raided English East Lothian and the Borders six times, burning Dunbar and overthrowing Melrose. Equally, in the other direction, Strathclyde Britons raided and burnt Pictish-controlled Dunblane in 840-50s. At this point Dunblane was probably called Civitas Nrurim, and was a major church centre. While there are only hints and traces remaining as to just how significant Dunblane was, there is more contemporary evidence for it than there is for Stirling. The key finds are two cross-slab frag-

---

independent rulers or perhaps even ancient king, whose territories eventually became Earldoms. Alex Woolf has argued that the word may be originally 'Sea-Steward' perhaps coming from Dalriada.

35   James IV has an English Queen, James V a French one; Mary Queen of Scots has first a French then a Scots husband, before she is overthrown in an English backed coup; James VI becomes king of England.

ments which are extremely rare survivals from a non-Pictish art tradition. These date to between 800 and 1000, and were found in the foundations of Dunblane's 12th century cathedral.

The pictured cross-slab is carved in relief on both faces and features both older pagan symbols and Christian motifs. The decoration on the cross recalls the one from Old Kilmadock, while the hunting scenes on the other side finds even more parallels in Pictland. The smaller fragment comprises a defaced cross-slab, which appears similar to the Northumbrian Crosses in Breedon, Leicestershire, some 300 miles apart. While these are not Pictish stones – as they don't have any Pictish symbols on them – they were clearly constructed when Dunblane was controlled by the Picts and may be an attempt to copy broader fashions. Certainly, they are proxies for power, skill and resources.

Another indication of the significance of Dunblane was that Kenneth MacAlpin's son King Aed was killed here in 878 by his own retainers, though the wider circumstances of the killing are completely unknown.[36] By this point there had been Viking raids across Britain for at least 80 years, getting ever bolder and moving from targeting island monasteries to deep penetrating destructive raids into the Pictish heartlands. This led to some of Columba's relics being moved from Iona to Dunkeld, and it's likely that a similar process led to St Blane's relics being moved from Bute to Civitas Nrurim (and its renaming to Dunblane – or rather Dol Blane). It is probably this that led to it being burnt down again, this time by the Vikings in 917 and may even have been raided after the Battle of Dollar in 875, when Aed's big brother, Constantine[37] lost to Healfdene.

The Viking and the Wolf[38]

---

[36]   As we shall learn, a similar cloak of mystery surrounds James IV's murderous coup against his father James III.

[37]   The contemporary sources describe his forces as both Picts and Scots, reflecting the period of transition.

• • •

These invading Vikings gradually settled in Scotland. While this tends to be associated with the Western and Northern Isles and Caithness,[39] there are Viking place names and burial monuments across the Forth Valley, so they settled there too.

The aim of all these invasions was to control the crossing at Stirling. While Stirling Castle rock may well have had an Early Medieval fortification, nothing of it survives and the only confirmed Miathian hillfort is Abbey Craig: an ancient volcanic fist, worn smooth but not down by glaciers. This incredible site lies under the National Wallace Monument (280942, 695621; 56° 08′ 18″ N 3° 55′ 03″ W) and comprises three ramparts, the inner of which survives to 1.5m high and 4m wide. Radiocarbon dates from the site indicate occupation between 560 and 968. It is entirely conceivable that at various times St Cadoc, St Serf, Nechtan, Urien of Rheged, Oswy, Trumwine, Kenneth MacAlpin and many other nameless heroes and villains all climbed this hill. Perhaps they journeyed in peace to feast, greet friends and cement alliances – or in anger to raid, steal

Abbey Craig vitrified rampart revealed for the first time in over 1,000 years

---

38   Another of Hector Boece's legends was that Stirling was saved from a Viking invasion by the howling of a wolf!

39   Orkney and Shetland would remain under Norse control until 1469, when they were part of the dowry for James III's Danish Queen.

and destroy. The fort may have heard recitations of the gospel, *The Strath Caruin Awdl* and *The Gododdin*, perhaps there were even lost tales of Emperor Septimius Severus and his terrible devastation.

Certainly, all of these raids and wars will have surged round this ancient spot – it's worth noting that both of Abbey Craig's inner ramparts are vitrified. The third outer rampart was rebuilt using vitrified material, i.e. after its destruction. Who was it built to defend against? Raiding Picts, Urien, Healfdene or the Strathclyde Britons? I'm afraid we shall never know. Remarkably, Abbey Craig appears to be one of the last hillforts ever constructed in what was about to become Scotland.

The Start of Scotland: AD 850 to 1000

So just as the Caledonians, Verutirones and Maeatae became Picts, Picts became Scots. But Scotland was still a small place, and the King of Scots continued to raid other kingdoms. In the late 900s Kenneth II (or Cináed mac Maíl-Choluim in Gaelic) had raided Strathclyde, Northumbria and The Lake District and captured the son of a Northumbrian King. However, he did not have it all his own way; he lost a battle – perhaps against Strathclyde in Flanders Moss (Moin Uacoruar) – and had to fortify the Fords of Frew, which were the Forth's lowest non-tidal ford. This lost frontier, an area fought and died over, can now be crossed at leisure (266852, 696034; 56° 08′ 18″ N 4° 08′ 39″ W). There is nothing there to mark its significance, though to the north it was controlled earlier by a broch (Coldoch[40]) and to the south by a hillfort: Keir Hill of Dasher. With the help of the owner Jeremy Gaywood, Kippen Heritage and the local primary school we dug here in May 2019 and dated it to 996-1153 AD, indicating it could have been visited or indeed built by Kenneth II.

To return to Kenneth II, his raiding yielded exceptional results and he seems to have been able to gain control of the Lothians, albeit at a price. Around 973, the Northumbrian King Edgar summoned the various kings of northern Britain (Strathclyde, Alba, The Isle of Mann and the Ilse's, Welsh and other Norse kings) to Chester to demand their loyalty, which was apparently granted.

---

[40]   Coldoch broch was the first ever broch to be ever excavated as a possible house. It was undertaken at the instigation of Christian Maclagan (who, being a woman, was ignored by subsequent accounts) by Sir James Young Simpson, the discoverer of chloroform.

Keir Hill of Dasher's ditch under excavation

To depart from our story a little, this question of over-lordship is always tricky. During the Wars of Independence, Edward I assembled anything he could find to boost his claim to Scotland. Along with the story of Albanus that we heard of earlier, these documents also revealed that MacBeth pledged allegiance to William The Conqueror, who may even have crossed at Frew. But (and this is a big but) by the time of the Wars of Independence Scotland's nobles were pledging all sorts of things and generally always going back on their word.[41] The reason was, of course, that Scotland was really hard to get to (remember that Scotland proper was to the north of the Forth – which means edge in Gaelic) and whatever you said in Chester stayed in Chester.

Slowly but surely the King of Scots strengthened his hold on the land south of the Forth. In 1018 at the Battle of Carham, Malcolm II and his ally Owain of Strathclyde raided deep into Northumbria, again probably crossing at Frew. This was a major victory for Malcolm who fundamentally destabilised Northumbria, leading to its collapse and pushing Scotland's boundary to The Tweed. In addition, Owain was killed, allowing the Scots to secure another vital possession – Strathclyde. But there was still really no Scotland, and nothing illustrates this more than Stirling's Burgh Seal.

If you live in Stirling or have visited you will have walked past several versions of it. This one is from Stirling's medieval Market Cross in Broad Street

---

[41] The one person who always remained true was of course Sir William Wallace, but more about him later.

The Burgh Seal, showing the Bridge Wallace used

(279325, 693710; 56° 07′ 15″ N 3° 56′ 33″ W). It illustrates two sets of figures fighting on Stirling Bridge. This is one of the oldest in Scotland and was first recorded at the surrender to Edward I at the Battle of Dunbar in 1296, when people from Stirling signed their seals on the Ragman Roll. Importantly, this is the only contemporary depiction of the bridge Wallace used. The current old bridge is only a mere 400-500 years old.

Anyway, round the edge of the seal is a Latin phrase: *Scoti stant hic cruce tuti hic armis bruti.* This is often translated as a wee poem: *The Britons stand by force of arms; the Scots are by this cross preserved from harms.* This is always taken to mean that there were both Scots and Britons in Stirling, and reflected a time when Stirling stood in the middle between the Kingdom of the Scots north of the Forth around Perth and Dundee and The Kingdom of Strathclyde (Britons). More recently 'bruti' has been translated as meaning brute so the phrase might mean *here brute Scots stand in arms, here safe in the cross.* This means that as late as the 13th century or perhaps within living memory, people in Stirling did not necessarily think of themselves as Scottish and indeed were quite happy to call Scots brutes. Indeed, they probably had more in common with Strathclyde than Dundonians. For the record I think Dundonians, Oor Wullie, the Broons and their bridies are all brilliant, and the V&A's not bad either.

Chapter Five

A New Millennium: AD 1000-1296

The Ceann Mor (Great Chief)

The Biggest Baddest Chief of them all: Mael Coluim mac Donnchada (Malcolm III): 1058-1093

As suggested by the assassination of King Aed by his pals, the history of these Kings of Alba was quite brutal and a lot of them ended up killing each other. What you won't know is that the kingship was passed between kindred (ie amongst cousins and brothers), not father to son[42] (which is of course known as primogeniture), as this allowed one branch of the family tree to accumulate too much power.

As you read on you will find that I think there are five truly great kings of Scotland, four of whom are obvious: David I, Robert The Bruce, James IV and James VI – and we will hear more of them later. However, the first great King of Scotland was David I's father, Malcolm III, and it was he who killed off kindred inheritance... along with quite a few people as well.

Malcolm tends to be overlooked because his son, in a classic Philip of Macedon way, simply outshone him. David I started a process known as the Davidian Revolution. Scotland was transformed by innovations from England: burghs, religious establishment, schools, coins and much, much more. With re-

---

[42]   Indeed, for a while during the earlier Pictish kingship father to son inheritance of kingship seems to have been explicitly forbidden.

gards to Stirling, David founded the burgh, the High School and Cambusken-neth Abbey, but all the groundwork was done by his father.

Malcolm III is the Malcolm from Shakespeare's MacBeth, who comes across as a bit of a fop: his opening line is to thank a wounded soldier bathed in blood for rescuing him. No one rescued the real Malcolm. Yes, he was in exile in England, but he, unlike any other king in Scottish history, was responsible for the death of his two predecessors (MacBeth and Lulach – and for good measure he also killed Lulach's son). MacBeth was a northern king with a base around the Moray Firth, and Malcolm's coup again shifted power to the south,[43] but this time it never went back and power remained with his children – who, as we shall find out, were every bit as ruthless as him.

Malcolm had two wives and 11 children. The first was a Viking Princess, Ingibiorg, while his second wife was Anglo-Saxon (Margaret[44]). It seems to be this second marriage that changed the scope of Malcolm's ambition: his first three boys were called Duncan, Donald and Malcolm – all good Gaelic names. But his second set of children were Edward, Edmund, Ethelred, Edgar, Alexan-der, Matilda, Mary and David – English, biblical or classical names. Malcolm III wanted his children to move in a broader world, to gain what was left of Northumbria, and barbaric Gaelic names would not help. He did manage to meet his ambitions and extended Scotland's borders to The Tees. While he did pay homage to William The Conqueror and his son William II, William I's new fortification at Newcastle underlined the weakness of the English hold on Northumbria. However, the English pushed back and a new castle in Carlisle cemented the new conquests, and Malcolm was killed on a retaliatory raid. As you might imagine, his death caused some problems – who exactly would inher-it?

Under Gaelic tradition the throne should have passed to Malcolm's brother Donald, but Malcolm favoured his second family. The result was three years of civil war and four different kings, with the English masterfully playing cousins, half brothers and uncles against each other. So the rather confusing suc-

---

[43]   This was the start of one of the fundamental shifts in Scotland. We moved further and further from our Gaelic origins with the Highlands and Is-lands becoming increasingly treated as barbaric and marginal. Resistance to this shift certainly plagued every king to James IV in 1493 when the Lord of the Isles sided with Henry VIII. And of course I've not included the Jacobites!

[44]   Margaret would become Scotland's only Royal Saint.

David I on Stirling High School

cession (pay attention) went: Donald III, then his nephew Duncan II, then Donald III again after a murderous coup against Duncan II, and then Edmund (another nephew) sharing power with Donald III. Edgar, the eldest of Malcolm III's second family, seized power from his uncle and half-brother. Edmund was secured with chains and sent to become a monk in Somerset while Donald III was blinded at the urging of David and imprisoned before being killed[45] on the orders of another nephew, Alexander, 10 years later. Phew! I really wouldn't want to attend any of their family Christmases.

The Margaretsons: some mothers do 'ave 'em: 1097-1153

It is a mark of the significance of Malcolm's second wife, Margaret, and their children that the boys are sometimes known as the Margaretsons in academia; something no other Scottish queen ever managed to do. Margaret was a religious reformer, and just before her death she asked for the help of the Archbishop of Canterbury to help reform the Cathedral at Dunfermline. This process, which was completed by her children, brought Scotland into the European mainstream of Catholicism and emphatically broke contact with the Columban mission of Iona. After this point Dunfermline would become Scotland's Royal Mausoleum, hosting 13 kings and queens (the last being Robert The Bruce) and again

Scotland's ancient Earldoms

---

45   Donald III was the last Gaelic King of Scotland and so it's entirely fitting that he was eventually buried in Iona, although he was the last ever King of Scots to be so buried, as the Norse soon cemented their hold of the west.

dragging the core Kingdom both south and east.

Edgar, Alexander and David all reformed Scotland; there are new castles, new institutions, new taxes and new Norman immigrants. These were all clearly attempts to bind the three disparate elements that the Kings controlled: Alba, Strathclyde and the Lothians. Edgar's charters are clearly written for a multiethnic kingdom, and even David's charters reflect different legal structures north and south of the Forth. An indication of just how significant Stirling was is given by the boundaries of Scotland's ancient Earldoms, which as we heard may have their origins in former kingdoms. The three to the west of Stirling – Lennox, Menteith and Strathearn – all have a curving eastern boundary with Stirling. This appears to reflect land carved from these ancient places that were to be controlled by the King, presumably someone between Kenneth MacAlpin and Malcolm III.

Edgar probably established the first Stirling castle, marking a break from the hillforts at Abbey Craig and Keir Hill of Dasher. However, he also formally conceded the Hebrides to the King of Norway as, again, he was more interested in focusing on the south. His brother Alexander established the Guildry in 1119, making it the third longest running institution in Scotland, after the crown and the church. Guilds were used by local merchants to control quality and ensure contracts were enforced; the cynical amongst you might even call them cartels. They were established by Royal Warrant and the crown extracted a fee for the privileges, i.e. the start of central taxation.[46] The symbol of the Guildry is the backwards '4' and you will see it all over Stirling if you pay close enough attention. Later members of the Guildry received a wee pie to give to their wives to prove they had attended the meeting (the qual-

A recently uncovered Guildry 4 on a gravestone

---

[46] An odd wee outcome of this medieval system was the Stirling Jug, the standard unit of measurement for liquids in Scotland from which all other units were copied. Edinburgh had the ell (for cloth), Lanark the pound, Linlithgow the firlot (for grain) and the reel (for wool). The jug was first recorded before 1437 and was only superseded by the Act of Union in 1707. The jug is now in the Smith Museum and it's worth noting that a Scots pint was three times larger than an English one - those were the days!

ity of the pies is not recorded). Alexander also founded a chapel in Stirling Castle around 1109, which is still there. He died in Stirling before being buried in Dunfermline.

David I took things much further and introduced Norman families into Scotland (The Bruces, The Stewarts – or rather their ancestors – and The Balliols, to name a few). As we've heard, he also established the Cambuskenneth Abbey and a wave of others, all of which revolutionised the economy, and he also produced Scotland's first coins. A similar economic innovation was the establishment of burghs which created mini-monopolies, again with the Crown charging for the privilege. All of this change – new people and new institutions – required donations of land, and he gave away so much that later on James I would describe him as 'ane sair sanct for the croune' (a sorry saint for the crown). However, David was very much a Keynesian King, and these investments yielded significant returns and boosted Scotland's economy. The charters also reveal a darker secret: amongst the parcels of land, the bogs (for salt), the fishing rights,[47] the timber, the income from ships and annual offerings of cheese we also find references to serfs or slaves. These people and their children were, in perpetuity, often part of the grant and indeed considered booty from warfare. During one of David's raids into Northumbria, local women were enslaved. However, slavery appears to have been abolished by the 1350s, although – as we shall see – it will raise its head again.

David managed to push Scotland's borders even further south, taking advantage of an English civil war known as The Anarchy, ostensibly to support his niece the then Queen of England. His Scotland had a core in the Borders; however, his gains were short lived and again the English border moved back north. In addition, he faced trouble from the west from Somerled, the first King or Lord of The Isles[48] and the north, where there were the descendants of King Lulach who had escaped his dad's attention. To make matters worse, there were a series of cousins and second cousins (descendants of Duncan II), and even an illegitimate nephew (the son of Alexander I). All of them were unhappy about the new changes, and all of whom had some level of royal blood and wanted a

[47]   In the medieval period Stirling was one of the main exporters of salmon in Europe, and the church's monopoly caused a lot of friction. Locals often destroyed their nets. Even after the Reformation there were still conflicts, and specific fishing courts were established to deal with disputes.

[48]   The current Lord of the Isles is Prince Charles.

share of power – because primogeniture was not yet standard practice. Of course as soon as it was, it caused big problems – as we shall learn.

While all these claimants would eventually bend the knee, they would outlive Malcolm III's line despite the most brutal of measures. For example, David ordered the blinding,[49] emasculation and imprisonment of Bishop Wimond, a grandson of Duncan II. Alexander II ordered the last of the MacWilliams, a baby girl, to be killed in 1230 by dashing her skull against Fofar Merkat Cross.

David's son Henry died unexpectedly in Northumbria and the kingdom was passed to his 12 year old grandson Malcolm (the last King of Scots with a Gaelic name), the first of many, many junior monarchs.

Kenneth's Bend or Muddy Creek?: Cambuskenneth Abbey: 1140 to 1560

The one thing still standing in Stirling from David's reign is the wonderful Cambuskenneth Abbey, although the only intact bit is the later bell tower, which is unique in Scotland. The grounds are open through the summer but not the full majestic height of the tower, as only the base is open. I open the tower once a year during Stirling Archaeology Month in September, and you must come if you're in town.

Now, our story will return time and time again to the Abbey, but let's

Two of Cambuskenneth Abbey's 13th century gargoyles

---

49   All this mutilation was fairly standard in Europe at the time and in some way considered less sinful. However, it was very gruesome and enemies of the Scottish crown had their eyes poked out, tongues cut out and were often castrated.

start with that name: *Cambus* is Gaelic for bend, so that's the lazy snaking meander of the Forth which surrounds the Abbey on three sides. The Kenneth might be Kenneth MacAlpin, or it might be something else garbled into Kenneth; we really don't know. I think the latter is probably the most likely option, as it underlines the nature of David's economic miracle. As we've heard, these early abbeys and monasteries were given two different types of resources: land and income. The founding charter from David for the Abbey included a fishing net, 40 shillings of the king's fees from Stirling, the income from one ship and one salt pit, and 20 cudermis[50] of cheese and lots of land. Most of this land was poor and boggy, but over centuries the monks transformed it into an economic powerhouse. However, this wealth led to corruption and the Reformation of 1560.

As the Abbey was surrounded by meanders, it had two access points from the river and one from land. From the east, access was along the Abbot's Great Carriageway, which linked the Abbey to both the Abbot's Palace at Throsk and the port at Airth. Parts of the road are still there and these lovely,

dark and deep woods are in fact the oldest oak avenue in Stirling. They date to the 18th century after the Abbey had long been abandoned but the land was still useful. As the road sits in the middle of the Stirling Highland Games ground, thousands of people walk here every year, but very few know of its significance. To wander this path is to walk with Abbots, Kings and Queens, heroes and invaders. If you left or arrived from the east in the Medieval period you would have passed the Abbey, and probably prayed for a safe return – or given thanks, if you were coming home. We know Robert The Bruce, James III and IV travelled here, but it's likely that Edward I and Mary Queen of Scots did so too, amongst so many others, including everyone who

The Abbot's Great Carriageway

---

[50]   I'm not entirely certain what a cudermis is (it might be connected to dermis for skin, so perhaps rind), and when I tried to ask for one in Waitrose they offered me a very nice dolcelatte which was great with pickled onions.

attended the first post-Bannockburn parliament which was held at the Abbey.

The road of course had to cross the Forth, and at this location there is a tidal ford which has been used since the Bronze Age. Literally thousands of people crossed here and, as we've heard, metal detecting here has recovered lost weapons as well as medieval and Roman coins. But the most famous journey was on the night of the 23rd of June 1314 when a renegade Scot, The Earl of Atholl, led a raid against Robert The Bruce's baggage train which had been stored at the Abbey. The scene is described by the first major poem in Scots, Barbour's *Brus*, written about 1375:

Cambuskenneth Abbey Ford: used for at least 3000 years

That he apon Saynct Jhonys nicht,
Quen bath the kingis war boun to fight,
In Cammyskynnell the kingis vittaill,
He tuk and sadly gert assaile
Schyr Wilyam off Herth and him slew
And with him men ma then ynew.

At the western end of the Abbey was a harbour or wharf which no longer works, as the river level has changed over the last 700 years – a fact which will become very important later on in the book. Returning to the tower, when you step inside, pause and let your eyes adjust – the stones in front of you are the remains of King James III's tomb, so don't climb on them. Above your head are three oblong holes for the bell ropes and, to your right, a locked door which is where my tour will take you.

A very rubbish lion

One of the highlights of the visit is this gruesome, if damaged lion. Look again and you can see the mane and those big giant paws, though the face and teeth are broken off. However, it has certainly been carved by someone who has never seen one. The best bit is the tiny wee human head, grasped between those ferocious piercing claws. Those eyes look like they are about to pop out from the crushing pressure of the paws. Given the relative proportions this would have had to be an absolutely massive, monstrous lion. It would also have been painted very bright colours.

The head in question represents a human soul, and the lion represents death. The motif is fairly common across Europe and has its origins in Roman times. It's either some kind of gargoyle or perhaps an element of a larger tomb. Certainly the Abbey had some very elaborate tombs, and had been re-endowed by James IV as a suitable setting for his father's tomb (James III) following his death at the Battle of Sauchieburn in 1488. His tomb was destroyed in the Reformation and later repaired by Queen Victoria.

James IV's role in his father's death racked him with guilt, and he took to wearing an iron belt as penance. This would have been extremely uncomfortable and was designed to scar and mortify his skin. It was James IV's intention to be buried with his father, although of course he fell at Flodden in 1513 and his body was never recovered. I suspect he commissioned the lion carving, but what did he think when he gazed at those terrible claws? Was he terrified that he would be dragged to hell?[51]

The lion sits in what we think is the scriptorium of the Abbey, where the documents were written and read. Now, where and when are you reading this book? Did you need to turn on a light? If you did, I take it that it was an electric one and not a candle? There was of course a time when we didn't have electric lights and candles were expensive. In the developing world, one of the factors that restricts children's education is the absence of light in the evening for homework. In a scriptorium each window has benches for sitting and reading, and those windows are really big. This was at a time when glass was really expensive, but writing was essential – and in order to write you needed light, so these massive windows maximised the amount of light during the day. One of things these monks scribbled in their records was a familiar wee rhyme:

---

[51] Certainly James appears to have viewed Stirling as a place for penance and his court poet, William Dunbar, complained that he would rather be in Edinburgh and urged James to:

'*Come hame and dwell no more in Stirling,*
from hideous hell come hame and dwell

Rumours that this is to be adopted by Edinburgh's tourist board are completely erroneous.

A loup o' The Forth,
Is worth an earldom o' the North

This was about how rich and fertile the farms where round here (another indication of David's wisdom) but it offers a tiny, precious, personal window into what our ancestors really thought. Such things are incredibly rare, as the majority of Scotland's past is silent. That's where archaeology comes in, of course, but it's a poor, mute substitute. What will any of us leave behind? What records will survive? Will anyone notice when we're gone? So make the most of the time you have, how you do that is up to you... personally I like to dig!

The Maiden, The Lion and The Red Fox-Cub: 1153-1248

The next three kings all have cool nicknames. Malcolm IV, 'The Maiden', the last Scottish king with a Gaelic name, believed in personal celibacy and pursued an idealised Arthurian path – and died a virgin. William I, 'The Lion', was known for his near-foolhardy bravery but was Scotland's longest lived medieval monarch. Alexander II's nick-name (The Red Fox-Cub) came from a taunt by the English King John because of his hair.

All of them had troubles with England. After losing his land in Northumberland, Malcolm volunteered for knightly service with the English king, thus implying Scotland wasn't an independent kingdom! William was captured by the English and only released after acknowledging England's feudal superiority (Edward I was very keen on this). Eventually he was able to buy his way out of it. Alexander II had more luck, and supported the rebels in the civil war that resulted in the Magna Carta.

All these kings faced rebellions from the usual suspects as they pushed and threatened for concessions, sometimes working with the king and sometimes against him. The kings also gradually turned their backs on the older ways, embracing French and English styles of dress and rule. Gaelic names vanished, and it was complained that Scottish kings *'were Frenchmen in race, manners, language and culture... they... have reduced the Scots to utter servitude'.* Slowly but surely the regional rivals became diminished. A good example is the family of Fergus of Galloway. Fergus was a powerful, semi-independent lord with connections to the Norse king of Man and Isles; some sources describe his descendants as kings. He and his descendants were key players in four kingdoms around the Irish Sea: Scotland, England, Man and Viking Ireland (to simplify a complex situation). Fergus witnessed charters for David I, but was deposed and replaced by his sons[52] who fought for the Scots, as did his grandson Alan who was a leading man in Alexander II's rule and even signed the Magna Carta. However, on his death his illegitimate son Thomas rebelled against Alexander III and would spend the next 60 years imprisoned. He was eventually released by Edward I during his conquest of Scotland. While he wasn't much use to Edward I, he outlived his enemy Alexander III by 10 years.

William and Alexander II had time to institute religious reforms, and William famously founded Arbroath Abbey. Alexander II introduced The Dominicans or Black Friars to Scotland, including one in Stirling, and the Black Friars helped Queen Margaret get made a saint.

Scotland's Sheriff Court: not the site of the 1180 assizes

In terms of Stirling, William had the biggest impact. He established The Royal Park, the oldest and best preserved in Scotland, and also started Scotland's first National Assizes, again in Stirling. And for good measure he died here, but was buried in Dunfermline. It is around this time that all this investment began to pay off. Stirling was a vital bridge to unifying the three core parts of Lowland Scotland, and was key to the creation of this brand new, very ancient place. With new legal structures come new names, and Alba began to be referred to as Scotland. This was not so much a change of status or identity but, as with Pictland to Alba, simply our elite rejecting Gaelic ways in favour of English and French. The English referred to Scotland, so that must be the most correct way – so Alba became Scotland.

Finally, it was Alexander II who agreed the border between Scotland and England and, while the country was nearly lost during the Wars of Independence, Alexander's border stands to this day.

---

[52]   One of the brothers blinded, castrated and cut out the tongue of the other!

Chapter Six

The Wars of Independence: 1296-1357

The Last Canmore and Beyond

Alexander III: 1249-1286

It was no doubt very hard for Malcolm III, with all his children, to imagine a time when his line would end. But in 1286 Alexander III plunged over the cliffs on his way to see his new wife, Yolande, dragging Scotland's hard won stability with him. His death and the decades of war that followed were lamented in an early Scots poem recorded by Andrew Wyntoun:

> Quhen Alexander our kynge was dede,
> That Scotlande lede in lauche and le,
> Away was sons of alle and brede,
> Off wyne and wax, of gamyn and gle.
> Our golde was changit into lede.
> Crist, borne in virgynyte,
> Succoure Scotlande, and ramede,
> That is stade in perplexite.

Certainly, things had not got off to a good start for Alexander III. He was seven when his father, Alexander II, had died while trying to invade the Western Isles. This was considered a divine intervention orchestrated by St Columba.[53] However, only fourteen years later, God had apparently changed his mind and, at The Battle of Largs, the Norwegians lost and Alexander III secured the Western Isles.

As the poem says, this enormous success marked what would soon seem like a golden age. Alexander III married Edward I's sister, Margaret, and they had three children – all of which was pointing to an inevitable Union of the Crowns. However, Margaret died in her twenties, as did all of her children (and their granddaughter, the Maid of Norway, would die soon after). This clearly prompted a change in tactics for Edward I, and Alexander's death at 43 gave him his chance. Scotland's nobility could not decide who had the best claim and behaved like a bunch of selfish children; there were raids and propaganda. Many of them appealed to Edward I to intercede, hoping that he would pick them. Edward I used the process to claim to be Scotland's feudal superior and when his appointment, John Balliol, refused to support his wars in France, he invaded in 1296 and launched over 60 years of conflict to control Scotland: The Wars of Independence.[54]

Under The Hammer: The Wars of Independence

As the Wars of Independence are amongst the best known periods of Scottish history, I don't really think you need to hear about them in detail from me. Instead I will focus on the following questions:

Why did we[55] win The Battle of Stirling Bridge?
Where exactly was the Battle of Bannockburn?
Who was the better leader: Bruce or Wallace?
Why did we win The Battle of Stirling Bridge?

Have you ever wondered why Wallace really won at Stirling Bridge? The story is very familiar: the English Commander John de Warrene[56] slept in

---

53   Alexander II's invasion was blamed on bad advice from Clement, Bishop of Dunblane and one of the first Dominicans in Scotland. Clement was also chiefly responsible for getting Queen Margaret beatified.

54   That 's' is very important: we Scots fought the English, the Irish, the Welsh and each other.

55   I can't deny that I'm Scottish and apologies to any English readers out there – but we did win, and we did it big style.

● ● ●
60

and ignored advice to avoid the narrow bridge, his troops advanced and then were recalled, eventually crossing again only to be surrounded on three sides by the Forth. When half the English army was over, Wallace blocked the bridge and the northern narrow point of the meander, trapping the English. The English command was split and poor; they had apparently expected us to wait for them to assemble before fighting. It just wasn't cricket...

The English army was amongst the best in Europe. It had just beaten the official Scottish army at Dunbar in 1296, and would beat us in again 1298 at Falkirk – and the English controlled Stirling Castle at the time of the battle. Yes, there was a small band of Scottish nobility on the English side of the river who were arguing for peace, and they joined in when Wallace was winning the battle. But this was an unofficial rebellion, our best position was the schiltron – a load of guys with big spears – we could not yet march, and yet we overwhelmed them. All they had to do was hold and wait and then they could have crossed the bridge and gone back to the Castle. Just to stress that marching bit again, the Scots were close to Abbey Craig and had to travel over a mile to the bridge. If they could not march, they would simply arrive as a bunch of individuals – so why did the English not just stand their ground?

Certainly the story of John Wright, the joiner who is supposed to have sabotaged the bridge so that it collapsed when the English were crossing, might explain the victory. This would clearly have split the English army, but why then did the other half not simply retreat to the Castle? Also, the English Commander of the Castle, Sir Marmaduke de Thweng (yes... that really was his name!), fled across the bridge – through his own men – so the battle was being lost before the bridge collapsed.

The Battle of Stirling Bridge is important in Scottish terms because it proved Scotland could win, and in European terms it was the first time an army of knights was beaten by foot soldiers. So how did Wallace do it? The English certainly couldn't explain it.

Sir William Wallace: The greatest ever Scotsman?

---

[56] It's worth noting that two Dominican friars were asked to negotiate peace between Warrene and Wallace.

As we've heard, excavations at Cambuskenneth's medieval harbour revealed that the Forth's contemporary tidal range was up to 2m higher at the time, which would have made it twice as wide, and remember all that mud – armour in metre-deep mud is useless. I think we won because the English panicked: they watched the tide rise and were trapped, people at the back were pushing forwards while those at the front were retreating, people fell into the mud and were drowned and crushed. If an army loses order, it's finished.

So Wallace won because the English panicked; they didn't know how high the Forth would rise and order broke down, with the resulting loss of 5,000 souls in the cold, clammy mud of the Forth – the best ally Wallace ever had.

Now what perhaps underlines the success of Stirling Bridge is the subsequent failure at Falkirk where, in theory, there was a plan. Wallace had the backing of the official Scottish state. We lost big time and, though it's true not all the nobility (including Bruce) helped, I'm not sure they could've done anything to avoid a defeat; remember they had failed at Dunbar. I also don't think Wallace really wanted to fight then and there; I think he wanted to draw the English ever further into Scotland and fight a long, drawn out, expensive campaign sapping morale and resources, but he was outmanoeuvred by Edward I. The Scottish army ended up being trapped and completely surrounded by the English forces, the foot soldiers and their schiltrons were no good against archers: they could not move and they were forced into a defensive rather than an offensive positon. It was a complete disaster.

Robert The Bruce: Scotland's greatest king (but not necessarily someone you would wish to invite for dinner)

Where exactly was the Battle of Bannockburn?

Now, sorry, but this is a trick question. There were two Battles of Bannockburn fought on two separate days in two separate locations. There are also at least two other major clashes and a series of massacres at pinch points after the conclusion of Day Two. Everything you think about Bannockburn is really about Day Two. The battles begin with a siege of Stirling Castle designed to force Edward into Scotland and undermine his support in Scotland. During Day One we stopped the English relieving the siege of Stirling Castle – that's it. Day Two was an absolutely incredible, outrageous victory. It was the most important Scottish victory in history. Remember, of course, both days were preceded by the systematic dismantling of English institutions in southern Scotland, stretching English supply lines and ensuring the campaign was ever more expensive (what Wallace was trying for at Falkirk). Bruce also stated he was coming to get Edward II's allies, forcing him to relieve the siege of Stirling Castle.

The reason for the debate over the location is twofold: firstly, we forgot very quickly where it was fought, and in 1488 James III thought he was fighting The Battle of Sauchieburn on the same field – he wasn't; secondly, the Victorians decided very confidently they knew exactly where it was and erected some monuments. These are at the core of the National Trust for Scotland Bannockburn Centre, which is all based on a dropped 16th or 17th century millstone (The Bore Stone) which is claimed to be where Bruce raised his standard. Despite the uncertain provenance, the romance and beauty of the spot had a big impact on Burns and it inspired him to write the great *Scots Wa Hae*. After this, a big flagpole[57] was erected and the Ordnance Survey decided that because The Bore Stone was there that the Roman Road must be close by and they marked it on a map. Then, because of the stone and the road and the flagpole, someone thought money could be made and a Custodian who sold postcards appeared. People started building houses nearby, and the site was under threat and had to be saved for the nation – enter the National Trust for Scotland. Once they had it, they noticed there wasn't very much to see, so history had to be improved. The Rotunda, the statue of Bruce and a memorial cairn were all erected in the late 1950s and 60s. All of which were revamped for the 700th anniversary.

But no-one has ever found the Roman Road. It could be closer to the modern road... we just don't know. Certainly Day One was fought roughly in this spot because to its east are a series of bogs,[58] which prevented the English flanking the Scots. The western flank was protected by both hand-dug pits and a then much larger Balquhidderock Wood.

Even more confusion surrounds Day Two. We know the English camp was on the carse between the Pelstream and the Bannockburn, and metal detection has identified battlefield objects there. But as well as the camp, this is also the area across which the English troops fled after the battle. The existing ac-

---

57 After the success of the Napoleonic campaigns there was a great deal of interest in 'Great' British battlefields.

58 Which, when drained, led to the discovery of the world's oldest curling stone, dated 1511.

counts discuss fighting taking place on firm ground and not the carse, implying that the English army had to march from the carse up the steep 50 foot slope to then meet the Scots.[59] The alternative is that the bulk of the fight was on the carse and that the English army's mobility was restricted by the ground conditions.

I have always favoured this latter option, as it implies Bruce planned for it. Certainly this was an enormous gamble; the English army was bigger and most had not fought the day before. The Scots also had to march and prepare overnight, so had little if any sleep after fighting all day. But what we are really talking about is the first clash of Day Two and not the main event, so does it really matter? It's either an astonishing Scottish victory or an absolutely astonishing Scottish victory. The English army failed to overwhelm and flank the Scots either because of the Scots' ferocity or the geography, or more likely a mixture of both. The critical factor was a brilliant innovation by Bruce: his schiltrons, unlike Wallace's, could move. They pushed the English cork back into the bottle of The Pelstream and The Bannockburn.

Traditional accounts suggest the Sma' Folk, or camp followers, were excluded from the main force and arrived later that day after seeing how the battle was going, panicking the English who thought they were a fresh army, turning a loss into a rout. Some are not certain that that they even existed; they might be a poetic conceit to demonstrate the whole of Scotland was on Bruce's side. They may even be an attempt to explain just how we won – again, does it matter?

Who was a better leader: Bruce or Wallace?

This might be rephrased to 'which was a better film: *Braveheart* or *Outlaw King?*' Both are brilliant and wrong; they take complex characters and times, and simplify them. So let me be clear: both Bruce and Wallace were violent killers, both committed savage acts – but only Bruce was excommunicated.[60] This

---

59   If you go to explore this slope, look for the large isolated wall. This is, in fact, the back stop for a rifle range. This appears to have been built or certainly became more popular during the French invasion scare of 1859 when Napoleon III rattled his sabre. Across Britain, the response to this was the formation of local militia. Intriguingly, one from Tullibody modelled its uniform on that of the Confederate army in the US Civil War.

60   The Bruces were definitely ashamed of Wallace's example, and Barbour's 'Brus' – the official account of the wars – makes no mention of Wallace.

was, of course, for the murder of his rival, The Red Comyn, under a flag of truce on holy ground. Wallace remained true to Scotland and was fighting for his country and his king. Bruce, his father and his grandfather fought for themselves; they twisted and turned with the political winds. My personal opinion is that Bruce extended the war by years

Scotland's greatest heroes: Bruce and Wallace

because he first had to unite Scotland at the edge of his sword[61] before turning it on England. In that light, Wallace was unquestionably the better man: he came further than Bruce, his rise was nothing short of miraculous, and there is no one else like him in Scottish history; indeed, his story is of international significance. I think he is poorly judged for his failure at Falkirk. He remained true and loyal, but some would say: so what? Bruce won, he had what it took, he is perhaps unique amongst Scotland's leaders: an absolute winner and clearly our greatest ever king. But was it Scotland that won or Bruce? Or did England simply lose interest?[62] Would we always have won? I will leave you to make up your own minds.

Robert The Bruce's only surviving son David II was not a very good leader and, while anyone might struggle in comparison with The Bruce, he really was a pale imitation of his father. He was captured by the English and offered them Scotland's throne if he could be released. Hmm... not a popular idea. He died without an heir, and seems to have been infertile.

But before we leave this period, a wee aside: I really wish objects could talk, or that we could invent some machine to reveal their stories. This tiny wee

---

[61]   Roughly a quarter of the nobles who signed the Declaration of Arbroath were plotting to overthrow him.

[62]   Remember, the key breathing spaces or treaties in the war were caused by changes in English leadership: Edward I died, allowing Bruce to cement his hold on Scotland; Edward II was deposed and then killed ahead of the 1328 Treaty, and Edward III was more interested in France and the 100 Years War.

A medieval bit of bling: worn by someone who fought with Wallace or Bruce?

thing is a decorative strap end, possibly from a belt or horse fitting. It dates roughly to between 1300 and 1400 and was found in the King's Park. We don't know who dropped it or their status, but given where it was found it was either someone employed by the crown to work in the park or someone enjoying the Park; the royal family or their aristocratic guests. It's quite plain, so if it was clothing we might imagine it was from a worker in the park, although if it was a horse fitting it's more likely to be from the elite. It was definitely dropped though, and was unlikely to be noticed until they got home and changed.

That date range is very important. It spans across both Scottish Wars of Independence, so it could have belonged to anyone of the thousands of different people in the armies of William Wallace, Robert the Bruce, Edward I or Edward II. Or someone from the English side, the English having controlled Stirling Castle twice over this period. It lay in the ground for over 600 years; it was repeatedly walked over, ploughed over, impacted by wind, rain, frost and ice, ignored and forgotten. A tiny wee survivor with a very big story that we will never, ever learn. Under Scot's Law, it's the property of the Queen (all metal detection finds in Scotland are), and the final part of its journey will be to the wonderful Smith Museum and Art Gallery where it will be preserved forever along with so many of Stirling's other treasures.

Chapter Seven

The Early Stewarts: 1371-1625

Founding a Dynasty

Robert II, Robert III, James I, James II and James III: 1371-1488

Bruce's daughter Marjorie married Walter The Steward and their son, Robert (later Robert II), founded the Stewart[63] Royal House. Now Robert was not a very loyal subject to his younger uncle David II,[64] and this seems to have started a trend for the next few years: duplicitous nobles who were frequently relatives. Robert II used his power to empower his sons who, as Walter Bower put it '*he maid rych and michty*', which of course created a series of rather large and serious unintended consequences. He faced a coup by his son, who was crowned Robert III and described himself as '*the worst of kings and most wretched of men in the whole kingdom*' and asked to be buried in a midden.[65] He was un-

---

[63]   Over time Steward became Stewart.

[64]   He had abandoned David II to capture by the English!

[65]   For those that like Thomas Hardy, this rather reminded me of The Mayor of Casterbridge's will:

'*That I not be bury'd in consecrated ground. That no sexton be asked to toll the bell. That nobody is wished to see my dead body. That no mourners walk behind me at my funeral. That no flowers be planted on my grave. That no man remembers me.*' Absolute, crushing misery.

dermined by his son the Duke of Rothesay and his brother Robert Duke of Albany. In turn Albany betrayed and imprisoned his nephew, Rothesay, letting him starve to death. His other nephew, the future James I, was captured while fleeing to France and held ransom by the English. His uncle, Robert Albany, and his son Murdoch, the next Duke of Albany, took their time getting his nephew and king released, and when James I came back he had Murdoch and his family executed for treason (Murdoch, his cousin, his two children and his father-in-law all fell to the axe). James I led a failed and ill-advised attempt to recapture Roxburgh, which was still in English hands; he panicked and fled, leaving his artillery behind. He was later stabbed to death in a blocked drain under a tennis court in Perth, in retaliation for the execution of various relatives.[66]

James I's queen, Joan, managed to survive the attack and then extinguished the male line of the assassin's family. James II stabbed The Earl of Douglas in Stirling Castle and then was killed by an exploding cannon in conflict with England, again at Roxburgh. The infant James III was kidnapped in an attempted coup, his brother supported an English invasion and he was killed in a coup led by his son, the future James IV, at the Battle of Sauchieburn. Although he did secure the

The Beheading Stone, where Murdoch Duke of Albany probably wasn't beheaded

Northern Isles for Scotland... as a wedding present! Phew... let's rewind a little.

An interesting wee fact is that while Bruce had Stirling castle destroyed after Bannockburn (to prevent it being used against him), it was rebuilt by the English during the second Wars of Independence and then recaptured by Robert II. This marked the castle's return as a significant centre. During David II's reign it started getting linked to Arthurian legend – it was called Snowden, and there was a talk of a round table. This reaches a peak during James IV and V's reigns; David Lyndsay's poem *Complaint of the Papyngo* is an example:

> *Adieu, fair Snowden, with thy towris hie;*
> *Thy chapel-royal, park and table round;*
> *May, June and July, would I dwell in thee,*
> *Were I ane man to hear the birdis sound,*

---

[66]   Is this perhaps the most bizarre death of any Scottish monarch?

Whilk doth against thy royal rock redound

In addition, we also know that Robert Duke of Albany died in Stirling Castle, and that James I's show trials were also held at Stirling; the official record of the latter event describes it as taking place on a hill beside the castle. In later years this has been connected to Mote Hill, also known as Murdoch's Knowe or Heiding Hill. Never one to miss an opportunity, Walter Scott included the hill in his blockbuster poem *The Lady of the Lake*, which helped to create the tourist industry (more about that later on):

> *'and thou, O Sad and Fatal Mound, That oft has heard the dread axe sound'*

Eventually some enterprising locals identified a big stone with knife marks on it in a local butchers and decided that this was the execution block used to behead Murdoch.[67] This was put back on Mote Hill (279323, 694475; 56° 07' 40" N 3° 56' 35" W) with a suitably impressive iron cage. This then proved to be a very popular post card (Google it). Now, another very odd consequence of *The Lady of the Lake* was the significant interest it generated in the Trossachs amongst the pre-Raphaelites... bear with me.

These lumps and bumps are all that's left of Old Kilmadock's[68] manse, which was demolished in the middle of the 20th century when the Council raised the level of the road and, in doing so, blocked access to the village! Anyway, the manse was where John Ruskin met his wife Effie Gray, who was Scottish and related to the minister. Ruskin was the most significant art critic of the 19th century and championed the pre-Raphaelites, although he was definitely a total weirdo. Now before any art historians splutter about my demeaning the great Ruskin, let me expand. Effie and Ruskin's marriage was never consummated and ended in

The remains of Old Kilmadock Manse where Ruskin first met Effie

---

[67]   Surely the steel of the axe would shatter on the stone?

[68]   The same one that's looked after by ROOK.

divorce. Effie later wrote to her father explaining the break-up was because Ruskin '*alleged various reasons, hatred to children, religious motives, a desire to preserve my beauty, and, finally this last year he told me his true reason... that he had imagined women were quite different to what he saw I was, and that the reason he did not make me his Wife was because he was disgusted with my person the first evening.*'

Yes, that's right – Ruskin didn't know what a naked woman looked like and was horrified by what he saw. In what was a giant Victorian scandal, Effie appears to have had an affair with John Millais, for whom she modelled at Brig o' Turk (for the painting *A Waterfall in Glenfinlas*), while married to Ruskin. The two later married and had children, and were even photographed by Lewis Carroll (author of *Alice in Wonderland*). And all that started at Old Kilmadock.

To return to that Arthurian theme, Allan's Primary School holds their annual sports day at Victoria Square garden; a very nice open space. As this is Scotland and the sports day takes place in summer, it's often cancelled due to rain. However, in March 1449 it would have been halted for a very different reason, for this was the royal jousting ground. James II was holding an elaborate and violent competition here, with Stirling Castle and its links to legend in the background. A very detailed account of the joust survives, and we know that much of the fighting took place between the Douglas family and French Burgundian knights, all watched by King James II. We know that the fighting involved lances, axes, swords and daggers until serious injury or death (or until the king had signalled 'enough'). There were lots of prizes: whoever broke the most lances; whoever hit their opponent on the head three times; whoever removed an opponent from his horse; and whoever stayed in the field the longest.

At the time the Douglases were jockeying for position and James was concerned that they were undermining him (remember his father, James I, had been assassinated). Famously this all came to a head at the Black Dinner of 22nd February 1452 in Stirling Castle, when James II murdered the 8th Earl of Douglas and

The pre-1500 jousting ground where the Douglases first annoyed James II

threw him from a window[69] (this is apparently the inspiration for the Red Wedding in *Game of Thrones*). Anyway, around 1500 James IV moved the jousting ground to the Butt Field, just below the castle, so it's all nice and quiet now. It's worth noting that an absence of interest in jousting, or rather the hoarding of money that it implies, was one of the reasons behind James III's fall.

As an archaeologist I prefer the testimony of the spade to history. In part this because there is so much to read but also because in general much of narrative history is, in part, a lie. Once you move beyond mere facts, i.e. the king died on this day at the Battle of Thingamajig, you end up mired in complex pieces of spin, accounts are lost or redacted, or simply never recorded. Someone is writing with one eye on justifying their own role or position. Or sometimes there is simply nothing – and this is the case with the Battle of Sauchieburn, 11th June 1488, in which the future James IV defeated his father James III, which led to James III's death. That's it – that's all we really know.

James IV, James V, Mary Queen of Scots, James VI: Peak Stewart/Stuart:[70] 1488-1625

The next four Stewart monarchs had an enormous impact on both Stirling and the whole of the British Isles. Indeed, one aspect of their legacies continues to have a global impact to this day. So James IV married Henry VIII's sister, but died at the Battle of Flodden[71]; their son married a French Queen, and their daughter was Mary Queen of Scots. Henry VIII became Protestant and tried to force Scotland to convert, and James V died from stress. Henry then tried to force the infant Mary Queen of Scots to marry his son by launching an invasion; this failed as Mary fled to France to become Queen. When Mary came back she was deposed. Her son, the infant James VI, was crowned, later also becoming James I of England after Elizabeth I died in 1603.

---

[69]   In retaliation the Douglases are said to have burnt down the town.

[70]   Stewart became Stuart after Mary went to France.

[71]   Flodden was the reverse of Bannockburn in terms of proportions. James launched an expensive raid into England, using weapons his troops had not trained with, on ground he did not know. His troops marched into a muddy hollow, they crushed each other and were massacred by the English.

Right, let's go back and revisit a few highlights. James IV was born in Stirling and conducted an awful lot of government business there.[72] He felt an enormous sense of guilt at his role in his father's death and embarked on a programme of penance. Simultaneously he also began to rebuild and renew Stirling Castle, building The Great Hall (the largest in Scotland), and the massive monumental gateway.[73] It's worth noting that from this version of the castle you could not see the town, as it simply spoiled the views. In addition, he appears to have funded research into flight, built Europe's largest ship (*The Great Michael*), reorganised the Royal Park and sponsored poets and playwrights. He married Henry VIII's sister, and the remains of their Royal Chapel are outside the church of the Holy Rude (279209, 693710; 56° 07′ 15″ N 3° 56′ 40″ W).

The Damian de Falcus bench, near where he fell

For me the most vivid details about this period are from the plays and the poetry. I quoted David Lyndsay earlier and another key poet was William Dunbar. In the poem *The Fenyeit Freir of Tungland*[74] he satirises John Damian de Falcus, an Italian abbot and alchemist operating in James IV's court, who conducts an experiment in flight by making a pair of wings. Needless to say, he fell to earth (or rather the castle rubbish dump) with a bang and broke his thigh. This bit describes the birds that pecked and swarmed John as he jumped from the castle walls:

Thick was the clud of kays and craws,
of merlins, mittanes and of maws,
That bickerit at his beard with blaws,
In battle him about:
They nibbit him with noyis and cry,
The rerd of them raise to the sky,

---

[72]   In terms of the top three locations for charters signed in his reign, it goes: Edinburgh (1475), Stirling (306), Glasgow (19).

[73]   This is described by a contemporary source as 'the four round towers of the four entries which is the whole outward beauty of the place'.

[74]   The Mad Friar of Tungland.

And ever he cried on Fortune, Fy.
His life was in to doubt.

Another interesting legacy of this royal focus on Stirling was members of the court donating money to good causes in the city.[75] Sometimes the sums were modest, as with the £20 (though this was a considerable sum at the time) given by Agnes Bowye, who was a royal laundress in the early 17th century. Others gave astonishing amounts. If you spend any time in Stirling you will learn that the area is full of spitals: Spittal Bridge, Spittal Street, Spitalmyre and Spital Hill to name but a few. But who or what was a spital, and is it any different to a spittal?

This is neither a poor tongue twister nor a cunning riddle. Spittal is named after Robert Spittal (or sometimes Spettal), James IV's tailor, who lived at Coldoch, and who also left money to the city.

Spital with one 't' is a contraction of 'hospital', which in medieval Scotland meant an almshouse or a religious centre where people could rest and be looked after. In Stirling the best known is Cowane's Hospital, which is the best preserved late-Medieval example in Scotland. John Cowane was a wealthy merchant in 17th century Stirling who left the equivalent of £3,000,000 to endow a charity which still functions to this day. Another example is Spital Hill in Causewayhead, which has been argued to be a Knight's Templar establishment, though the Holy Grail isn't there (I've looked).

Robert Spittal's Trust

The image is of a memorial stone from Spittal's Hospital (or Spittal's Spital), visible on the Back Walk. The 'Liberal man' quote is from the Bible and is connected to generosity of giving and not party politics. The scissors are the symbol of the tailor. What is particularly interesting are the two sunken oblong holes; these are likely to be corrections from a mistake by the mason, though which James he had he put up first and when the mistake was noticed we shall never know, but I bet there was some swearing involved.

---

75   It wasn't always a good thing; one Jonat Tenant had to wait eight years before being paid by Mary de Guise.

Spittal's money arguably did more good than Cowane's, as we have two Spittal Bridges, one at Doune and one at Bannockburn, along with an almshouse which eventually became the site of the old High School on Spittal Street.

Following the death of his father James V was crowned in Stirling Castle in the chapel Royal, and he too loved being in Stirling and spent most of his Easters there.[76] He is responsible for the magnificent Stirling Castle Palace, one of the finest Renaissance palaces in Britain. James, his wife Mary of Guise and their daughter Mary Queen of Scots, mark the last bright gleam of Catholic Scotland and the peak of French influence. Like his uncle Henry VIII he was very keen on jousting, and built a new road from the castle to the new jousting grounds that his father had developed. This was called Bog's Passage, and was built in 1531 for £5 – surely Scotland's cheapest ever road. It still stands today, and I uncovered some of it during a path upgrade. Oh, the exciting life of a Council Archaeologist.

Bog's Passage: the cheapest road in Scotland

Famously James V was known as the Guidman o' Ballengeich. Ballengeich Road (279075, 694060; 56° 07′ 26″ N 3° 56′ 48″ W) is a lovely but very steep road round the north side of the castle. The name is clearly Gaelic in origin, *Bal* tends to mean village, but in this case the name is often interpreted as 'windy pass'. But to return to James, he got that nickname because according to legend he used a small track down to Ballengeich Road to have various adventures[77] in disguise amongst his subjects. The picture here is the northern Castle gate, the one probably used by James V. It's at the top of a very steep slope full of brambles. It was designed to allow small numbers of troops in and out during sieges, and was known at the Sally Port (from the French 'saillir', to surge through, while 'port' is of course gate). There is another one on the south side, but it's covered by ivy. The Sally Port itself seems to have been sealed in 1689 when the

---

[76] The top three places where documents were signed were Edinburgh (1475), Stirling (436) and Falkland (198).

[77] These adventures didn't always end well and James once accidentally killed the Park Keeper's wife's cow with a gun.

The Sally Port

outer defences were strengthened. It's marked by a wee sign on the inside of the castle but there's nothing to say whether James V really used it or not – though I like to think of him chuckling to himself as he crept out of the castle in disguise to have some fun in Stirling.

Following James V's death, Mary was crowned, like her father, in Stirling Castle – yet another infant monarch. To stop the English forcing Mary to marry Henry VIII's son ('The Rough Wooing'), we built Stirling's city walls. Now these are famously the best preserved in Scotland, although they really only run around the southern face of the city, the idea being that boggy ground to the north would stop any army. Also, there seems to have only been one formal gate;[78] the rest just seem to have been gaps that were blocked in times of trouble.

Now, as you all know, Mary was of course deposed, in part because she was Catholic and we were moving towards Protestantism. It was also clear that the French supported her, which annoyed the English-backed Protestants, and finally she was strongly suspected of being involved in the death of her husband Darnley, who of course was James VI's father.

This new religion of Protestantism was a rather severe affair and Stirling's Presbytery records from the 1580s show ministers banning bonfires at mid-summer,[79] being shocked at dancing

A bastion on Scotland's best surviving city wall

---

[78]   This is where Wallace's arm was supposed to have been nailed, though it's more likely that it was displayed at Stirling Bridge.

[79]   This was probably a hangover from the Celtic festival Beltaine, which survived outside Callander until the late 18th century. Also, Dunblane contains the one surviving Beltaine place name left in Scotland. It was applied to a standing stone (the Beltaine Stone) currently known as the Gathering Stone (281093, 702182; 56° 11' 50" N 3° 55' 05"

on the Sabbath, banning pipes and fiddles at weddings, and hunting for any re-maining Catholic practices. Even as late as 1699 someone was brought before the kirk session for gardening on Sunday. Ah, does it not feel good to do The Lord's work?

The main intellectual force behind Mary's deposition was her former tu-tor, George Buchanan, one of Europe's finest Latin poets and a victim of the Spanish Inquisition. George was born in Killearn, which lies to the west of Stir-ling. Following Mary's downfall, there was a brief but bloody civil war. The Regent for the infant James VI was his grandfather, Mathew 4th Earl of Len-nox. On the 4th of September 1571 outside Mar's Wark (279228, 693747; 56° 07' 16" N 3° 56' 39" W),[80] there was a violent struggle with Mary's supporters and Mathew was shot and died of his wounds within four hours.[81] While early re-ports suggested he was killed by his own men, the blame was eventually placed – rightly or wrongly – on Mary's shoulders. Of course, this meant James' moth-er could be accused of the death of both his father and grandfather; not a recipe for a happy childhood.

Now for any tourists reading this I can reassure you that Stirling's streets are currently free of gun-toting assassins. Indeed, guns are very rare sights these

A mermaid on Mars' Wark

W). Some 'witches' even confessed to dancing round fires at Beltaine with fairies.

80   It's worth spending a good few minutes looking at this incredibly richly carved building which features corpses, green men and mermaids!

81   A few years later in 1578 another high ranking official, Lord Glamis (an ancestor of the current Queen), was also shot in a brawl in Stirling, alt-hough apparently this happened as he was too tall, which to be fair was not a common problem in Medieval Scotland.

days, yet the evidence for their use and the threat of them is all around Stirling. There are impacts from musket balls at Cambuskenneth Abbey, the Church of the Holy Rude, St Ninians Kirk and the Castle. Older buildings like Mar's Wark have gun-loops in the front (so you can shoot at people); always handy if you're trying to defend the head of state – though we heard how that went.

But where did all these guns come from? One of the surprising locations is Doune, which had an international reputation for gunsmiths. It is even said that the first shot of the American Revolution was from a Doune pistol. The industry started with Thomas Caddell, who started making pistols in 1646. They were sold in pairs and were both deadly and attractive, and there was a weekly sale at the Market Cross. One of the original pistol factories is just off Main Street (272802, 701557; 56° 11' 23" N 4° 03' 04" W). The gun trade gradually fizzled out in the late 18th century as the scale of production got larger, although there was still a gunsmith working in Baker Street in Stirling in the 1820s. Doune pistols are currently highly sought after by collectors.

The King James Bible

What is the most popular version of the best-selling book of all time (though have you ever tried selling one)? Most of us don't own one but our grandparents probably did, and most of us have probably never read it, though there's a copy in every British and American hotel room you have ever stayed in. I am of course talking about the King James Bible, which has its roots in Stirling. The James in question was King James VI, who was Scotland's first Protestant monarch, crowned in our very own Church of the Holy Rude, in a service by John Knox, after his mother's deposition.

James was strictly tutored in Stirling Castle by the formidable and elderly George Buchanan, who as we've heard also tutored his mother.[82] Indeed, so severe was his schooling that James was terrified by the memory of his former teacher and no-

The dreaming spire that influenced James VI: The Church of the Holy Rude

---

[82]   His nephew was also a teacher in the town.

tably Buchanan is reputed to have said to King James' courtiers that while '*you may kiss his arse, I hae skelped it*'.

The new bible was composed to deal with inaccuracies in older versions, and of course a bible that people could read without knowledge of Latin was one of the central tenets of the Reformation. James was still King of Scotland when he first proposed the idea, but being King of England gave him the resources to propose this revolutionary project.

It's hard to describe the overwhelming influence of the King James Bible, but perhaps the most telling compliment comes from arch-atheist Richard Dawkins who says that '*a native speaker of English who has never read a word of the King James Bible is verging on the barbarian*'. Why not see if you have a copy lurking somewhere? If nothing else, it's worth reading to see what all the fuss is about![83]

Silenced Generations

While we know far more about medieval people than we do about their prehistoric ancestors[84], we still don't really have a good picture of them. They're vague and blurry compared to our current world. We do know that most of them were farmers, but farming was very different and didn't use ploughs, which turn the soil over; it used ards, which break soil up. Ards were pulled by oxen, not horses which were and are expensive beasts, prone to damage to their ankles – oxen are much tougher and cheaper. They worked long linear fields full of rig and furrow (or ridge and furrow as it's known in posh circles), which Scotland was once covered in. The picture shows medieval rig and furrow

Medieval agriculture on Gowan Hill

---

[83]   Though, of course this version changed the meaning and significance of certain passages and one of the more interesting edits was the removal of female metaphors for God, which are still in the Talmud. James absolutely considered God male, no shadow of a doubt; perhaps his view of his mother coloured this.

[84]   In fact we know more about the last few seconds while you read that line than we do about the first 9500 years of Scotland's history.

surviving on Gowan Hill (279177, 694329; 56° 07′ 35″ N 3° 56′ 43″ W) at the heart of James IV's Royal Park. What you did was dig a trench and pile the soil from the trench to the right, and on the other side of the mound you dug another trench and put the soil to the right, and so on and so on – and this is what you planted in. The soil here was deeper and had two drainage gullies to either side which provided slightly more favourable growing conditions.

This form of farming was hard work and gave low yields. It was replaced from the late 1700s by the square fields we know today, which were much more efficient but destroyed most of the earlier the rig and furrow. Because of this and other changes, through the late 18th and 19th century Scottish agricultural output increased by around 300% – an economic miracle. But where did all the people go? Well, they left to work in the new factories in the cities, and this is known as the Lowland Clearances. Landowners attempted to gain the same economic returns later on in the Highlands... albeit with far more brutal methods.

Chapter Eight

The Modern Era: 1603 Onwards

Twilight of the Stuarts and Beyond

The Last Stuarts: Charles I, Charles II, James II (or VII)[85] and Bonnie Prince Charlie: 1625-1746

The 25th of July 1603 was a very momentous day for Scotland – our King, James VI, became James I of England. Now, whatever the ins and outs of the Union of the Crowns, this was absolutely calamitous for Stirling which went from being one of the most important places in Scotland to a regional backwater. The money began to leave, and Stirling began to decay. By the late 18th century there were abandoned and collapsing houses, the incredible renaissance carved heads in James V's magnificent palace had fallen off, and the building was stripped to be converted to a barracks. As Burns angrily put it in a very risky poem[86] inscribed on a window in the Golden Lion a hotel in Stirling (still open today):

> *Here Stewarts once in triumph reign'd,*

---

[85] No one ever talks about Charlie's father and I won't either, as he doesn't seem to have done anything!

[86] He had arrived within 10 years of the conversion and the poem, with its seditious tone haunting his later life, and he revealed that he had been *'...questioned like a child... and blamed and schooled for my... Stirling inscription'*.

And laws for Scotland's weal ordain'd;
But now unroof'd their Palace stands,
Their sceptre's fall'n to other hands;
Fallen indeed, and to the earth,
Whence grovelling reptiles take their birth.
The injur'd STEWART-line are gone,
A Race outlandish fill their throne;
An idiot race, to honor lost;
Who know them best despise them most.[87]

The last major royal investment in Stirling was the construction of King's Knot for the coronation of Charles I. There had always been something in the location, and it was the likely home of the Round Table mentioned in earlier poetry. By the time the King's Knot was proposed, the older garden was covered in brambles and was a bit of an eyesore so it was definitely time for something new. At the centre there would probably have been a fountain or a sundial. The garden was designed and built by English gardener William Watts who was described as '*skilfull and well experimented*' and for all this wonderful work was paid just £30 a year (can I get him next?)! Despite Stirling's loss of influence through the 17th century the garden was never ploughed up, but just turned over to grazing – leaving us with, as one expert describes it, the finest lost garden in Scotland.

The King's Knot: Scotland's finest lost gardens

It's a just a lovely park now, known locally as the cup and saucer. In Easter children roll eggs down it,[88] and in winter we take sledges down its steepest side and on a clear day the view to the hills is just incredible.

---

[87]   A slightly later, more romantic and less angry version of the same sentiment was penned by James Hogg:

'Stirling... but I love thee more
For the gray relics of thy martial towers,
Thy mouldering palaces and ramparts hoar'

[88]   My daughters stopped rolling theirs and just eat the chocolate now, which lasts for months and months – yet there's never any for me!

• • •

82

As you might know, Charles I ended up getting his head chopped off for trying to subvert Parliament. Cromwell took power, and after his death Charles II reclaimed the throne.[89] After *his* death, his brother James II (or VII of Scotland) took over and he in turn was deposed, being replaced by his nephew and daughter, William and Mary. Then Mary's sister, Anne, became the last Stuart monarch. Bonnie Prince Charlie was James VII's grandson, and his bid for the throne ended at Culloden in 1746. Now, as we shall learn, this conflict was to do with two key factors: various strands of Protestantism versus Catholicism, and the right of individuals to worship as they saw fit without state interference.

Before we go on, it's worth noting that from the 17th century the nature of Scottish historical records starts to change. There are many more sources such as court records, wills and many more books, making names, lives and crimes all more visible and tangible. For the first time history records significantly more of the smaller, mundane and personal. Perhaps the most personal source of these stories are gravestones, and the most common symbols on 17th and 18th centuries were skull and cross bones.

In the past there were no restrictions on how many people could be buried in a cemetery, and so gradually the ground level increased in a process called grave creep. When you dug a new grave, you inevitably disturbed the previous occupant – or as John Donne put it:

No pirates be here

> *'When my grave is broke up again
> Some second guest to entertain'*

This re-excavation of older graves disturbed older burials, and these disarticulated human remains are known as charnel (hence 'charnel house'). The most recognisable elements are skulls. Famously, in Shakespeare's *Hamlet*, he passes a newly-dug grave and picks up a disturbed skull and says '*Alas, poor Yorick...*' After skulls, the long bones of legs and arms are the most recognisable. So skulls and long bones were depicted on grave stones to remind mourners that

89   An odd wee aside connected with Charles II's visit to Stirling in the mid 17th century is that he was able to draw on medieval laws requiring all 'strangers' to leave the city.

they too will die and end up as bones (so repent, time is running out), which of course leads to depictions of hour glasses that you might also spot in a cemetery. Given the association with death, this may have led pirates to adopt the symbol and of course it currently appears as a warning on toxic substances. But there are no pirates or toxic substances in Stirling cemetery, and so no reason not to visit it.

The 17th century is perhaps the most complex, divisive and bloody period of Scottish history (it culminated in The Killing Times), and those fissures are still present today. However, I can think of no other spot in Scotland that connects these themes with so fierce a vitality as Stirling's Old Town Cemetery (of which, incidentally, William Wordsworth said he knew of '*no*

Stirling's Old Town Cemetery

sweeter cemetery in all our wanderings'). There are actually four different parts to it: the higgledy-piggledy medieval cemetery; the ornate Victorian Valley cemetery with the statues of Protestant reformers and martyrs; the Drummond Pleasure Ground with the pyramid; and the 20th century Snowden Cemetery.

At the centre of the Old Town Cemetery (279099, 693778; 56° 07′ 17″ N 3° 56′ 47″ W) there is a very prominent wee knoll called Ladies Rock. This has

Ladies' Rock: one of the most accessible and best views in Scotland

one of the best 360 degree views in Scotland. To the west, Ben Lomond and the Carse; to the north, the castle and Ochils; to the east, Stirling and the broad flood plain of the Forth and to the south trees.[90] Over the centuries you would have been able to spot a number of incredible events from this vantage point. In the distant past you may have seen whales swimming past and our earliest

---

90   Which were planted in the 19th century under protest by the military in case they provided cover for invading troops – clearly Stirling Castle was all that stood in the way of a hostile invasion!

ancestors walking along a lost shore; lines of Rome's legions; hordes of raiding Picts, the smoke from the destruction of Mote Hill; the march of William the Conqueror to meet Malcolm III; the construction of Alexander I's chapel; Edward I's great War Wolf and destruction of Stirling Castle in 1304; and one of the first set of firework displays in Scotland for the future James VI's baptism.

In the 17th century you might have seen the burning of witches or soldiers exchanging fire in the graveyard during Cromwell's siege of the Castle, which

left their mark on the cemetery's second oldest gravestone: The Service Stone. In January 1746 you would have had to fight for space as Bonnie Prince Charlies' troops erected a gun emplacement for the last ever (futile and failed) siege of the Castle, the exchange of fire damaging the nearby Mar's Wark where James VI's grandfather died from his fatal shooting.[91]

The current view features lots of impressive statues and Scotland's largest urban pyramid. These were all meant to provide noble examples to Victorian society, and replaced what had become a bit of a drinking den (or so the reformers claimed). Gardens like this were designed to provide not just a nice walk but an edifying example to wider society; these statues were of role models. They were primarily aimed at the working classes so that they had something to do in their free time other than merely drinking and watching football.

The impact of war: 17th century musket ball impacts

The Pyramid is known as either Salem Rock or the Martyr's Monument, or the Star Pyramid. It's the main feature of Drummond's Pleasure Ground, and is dedicated to all those who suffered martyrdom in the cause of civil and religious liberty in Scotland.[92] This and the Valley Cemetery were mostly funded

---

91   The author of *Gulliver's Travels*, Daniel Defoe, had visited it in 1723 and worried that it might be damaged as it was too close to the Castle. It was still ruinous in 1752 and was used by James Kirkland to hide a pistol and gloves that he had just stolen!

92   I made a very small contribution to a TV programme called *Heavenly Gardens*, which I thought was great fun – but they really didn't want to

by the Drummond family. Their money came from seed merchants, though they also expanded into publishing. All of the statues in the cemetery – also funded by the Drummonds – are to leaders and martyrs of the Church of Scotland, all individuals who put their views on the worship of God above all else.[93]

Salem Rock: a monument to religious and political freedom

The statues include: Knox, who led the Reformation in the 16th century; Erskine, who broke away from the main church of Scotland in the late 18th century over issues of patronage (i.e. who appoints a minister[94]); and the Solway Martyrs, two women (Margaret McLachlan (63) and Margaret Wilson (18)) who were tied to stakes in the Solway Firth by the state and left to drown as the tide rose.[95] Also featured are James Guthrie and James Renwick, the first and last Church of Scotland ministers, killed by the state during

---

hear about 17th century Covenanters and their tendency to take up arms in defence of their freedoms!

93   From the point of view of people in Stirling in the late 19th century, God was white, Protestant, and it was their burden to bring this Good News to the world via the British Empire – frequently at the end of a gun.

94   These intellectual fissures would emerge again in 1843 when the Free Church was formed. Unfortunately some of these 'free' churches were built on tainted money from American slave owners. Frederick Douglass (who adopted that name after hearing Scott's 'Lady of the Lake'), the ex-slave and advocate for freedom, spoke across Scotland and demanded that they 'send the money back'. While he never spoke in Stirling (the train connections were better in Falkirk) another ex-slave, Moses Roper, spoke all over the area. Moses had been left in slavery by his white father and was then sold 17 times and severely tortured after repeatedly trying to escape.

95   I must apologise here to readers of my first book; I was so horrified by this story and a slightly misleading secondary source that I thought it was propaganda... but it's not.

The leaders of the Scottish Reformation

the Covenanting Period, the core of which is known as The Killing Times, when over 100 ministers were killed.

What the...? The Scottish state executing people for their religious beliefs? It's a complex issue that I'll only just touch on briefly here. Basically, Charles I, Charles II and James VII were quite big on central authority and wished to control how people worshipped. These authoritarian tendencies led to Charles I being executed. The Scots then backed Charles II in an invasion of England to regain his throne on the basis of guarantees of religious freedom (The National Covenant) which led to the Covenanters. They lost the Battle of Dunbar[96] and Cromwell invaded, establishing the Commonwealth.

At Charles II's restoration he reneged on his agreement and imposed his preferred style of worship on Scotland. Ministers objected to this and some even took up arms against the state (e.g. James Ure of Kippen), while others held outdoor worship meetings called Conventicles. The state organised increasingly brutal repression of these events, ministers were killed and went on the run, and some even adopted disguises.[97] All of this ended in 1689 in what is called the Glorious Revolution, but more about that later on.

---

[96]   Now, many of those captured by Cromwell's army (Scots and Irish) were sent to the colonies as indentured labour. This was clearly a form of slavery, but it was not the same as the enslavement of African and other peoples. Yes, the Scots and Irish prisoners had no choice, but Cromwell's slavery (or rather indentured labour) ended at some point. For Africans and many others it did not end, and their children were conceived in bondage and born as property.

[97]   The son of one minister, John Blackadder, who died imprisoned on The Bass Rock, later became the Governor of Stirling Castle, clearly demonstrating the changing political winds! When John's diary was first printed it showed him with a dark skinned child, possibly a servant or perhaps a slave, who was edited out of the later editions.

I'd like to drill down a bit into all of this. James Guthrie had been the Minister at the Church of The Holy Rude, and after his execution his head lay on a pike in Edinburgh for 27 years. Cromwell described him as the '*small man who would not bend*'. He had actually been kicked out of his church by the congregation for not being radical enough. This of course meant that he missed out on Stirling's largest ever witch trial, which took place in

The first minister to be executed by the British state: James Guthrie (279183, 693760; 56° 07' 16" N 3° 56' 42" W)

March 1659. This dubious honour fell to his deputy, one Mathias Sympson, and may I say that I hope he's rotting in hell.

Do you believe in witchcraft? For the record I do not, but our ancestors certainly did. They believed that the Devil was an active force of corruption, always trying to tempt people, and that witches were his agents on earth.

Before modern medicine anyone practising folk remedies might fall under suspicion and, of course, could always be denounced by a neighbour who they fell foul of. In Stirling there were always more trials for false accusations than for witchcraft itself. But witches were thought real because even the King believed they were. James VI believed he had survived an assassination attempt by North Berwick witches. He wrote a book about demons and was actively involved in the interrogation of a poor woman from Stirling who had been freshly pricked. The pricking of a witch involves repeatedly jabbing them with a bronze pin until you found a point where no pain was felt:

St Ninians Well: the scene of a confessed act of 'witchcraft' (279684, 693014; 56° 06' 53" N 3° 56' 12" W)

this was where the devil[98] had supposedly touched the witch to seal their bargain.

Of course this is why Shakespeare's only Scottish play, *MacBeth*, deals with witchcraft and indeed James makes a cameo in it, although his mother Mary, Queen of Scots explicitly doesn't. The witches in the play are concerned with overthrowing the state and corrupting good heroic men and women. They speak in riddles and half-truths, using MacBeth's ambition and strength against him; their Goddess Hecate promises to confuse him, and:

> *'Shall raise such artificial sprites*
> *As by the strength of their illusion*
> *Shall draw him on to his confusion'*

Now that last bit is important. A 17th century 'witch' was not what we would understand today as a wiccan. There were certainly people who practiced healing or believed in 'magic', but they would not have called themselves witches. Indeed, some of these healers[99] included phrases from the Bible in their chants to demonstrate that they were not evil. To be called a witch then was, socially, like being called a paedophile today. That is not to say that there were not people who really thought they were witches. For example, Margaret Duchill, who was tried in Alloa in 1685. She was described as an unrepentant witch; she was said to have wanted the Devil's power to smite her enemies and claimed to have killed several people and animals. As witches were and are not real, precisely what happened is unclear: but she apparently claimed to have slept with the Devil. Did she dream this, or was she subject to a horrible and cruel trap by a local man? Perhaps she was mentally ill, or her confession forced? Other witches seem to have believed they flew or achieved other incredible feats. Isobel Gowdie claimed to have yoked frogs to a plough to destroy the fertility of a field; other times she said she had broken into houses to steal food and

---

[98]　Those engaged in interrogation were curiously obsessed with the Devil's penis, and it transpires that those 'witches' who supposedly encountered it described it as 'ice cold'.

[99]　But even folk healers still believed in magic. For example, Marjorie Wingate in St Ninians got into trouble for collecting water before sunrise, as dawn would have dissolved the magic. Another 'witch' confessed to performing magic in St Ninians Well, pictured above.

drink, refilling barrels with her urine.[100] Some have claimed that these were the fertile imaginations of repressed people, broken under torture. Others have argued that these may be vivid dreams or hallucinations brought on by regular deprivation and hardship, the regular and typical lot of peasants. Certainly the only real acts of evil were those of their interrogators.

To return to the Covenanters, the Kippen Minister, James Ure, led 200 volunteers from Stirling to the Battle of Bothwell Brig in 1679. Following their defeat, Ure went on the run in the hills above Kippen and stayed at the Hole of Sneith. A reward of £100 was offered for his capture, but no one betrayed him.

His mother was arrested and died in Glasgow Tolbooth, while his wife and young child were held for questioning for four weeks in the Edinburgh Tolbooth. As noted above, all of this was forgiven after William of Orange came to power in 1689 (in what is known as the Glorious Revolution) and former religious extremists (or freedom fighters) became members of society again. Now, this Dutch-backed coup resulted in the deposition of James VII (the last Catholic monarch of Britain) and led to systematic repression of Catholics.[101]

The amazing geology around the Hole of Sneith (265613, 693156; 56° 06 ' 44" N 4° 09 ' 46" W)

The attempts of the Catholic Stuarts to regain the throne would end at Culloden in 1746.

However, 1689 was neither bloodless nor without opposition. We have heard that James V's wee passage was sealed around by this time and troops were rushed to control that *disaffected town of Stirling*. The resulting Civil War was brief but confusing, and no one encapsulates this period more than

---

[100]   Similar events are described in James Hogg's poem The Witch of Fife, albeit with a much more comic tone. It starts with a suspicious husband demanding to know where his wife was going each night, and then moves to him being jealous of his wife's hijinks. He then joins the witches in their fun, mainly getting drunk on the Bishop of Carlisle's wine and it ends with her rescuing him from his drunken foolishness.

[101]   In turn this resulted in the Orange Lodge, the Billy Boys and in America – Hillbillies.

John Graham 1st Viscount Dundee who has two main nicknames: Bloody Clavers and Bonnie Dundee. The first name was given to him by the oppressed Covenanters, who he harried and imprisoned on behalf of James VII – who he remained loyal to ever after his deposition. He achieved a series of stunning victories, but was ultimately killed and the Glorious Revolution rolled on – this is why the Jacobites called him Bonnie Dundee.[102]

Attention to details, and ever more personal stories

As we progress through the 17th century there are ever more documents and thus ever more details about people's lives or rather about how horrible they were. People often ask me when I would have most liked to have lived, and I always give the same answer: now. Life in the past was '*nasty brutish and short*', yes, it might be fun to watch the Roman Legions march past Stirling, but they are likely to have sold me into slavery and they would have been far less delicate with women and children.

Nothing speaks more eloquently about how brutal the past was than the punishments, all of which were decided in the Tolbooth (279305, 693683; 56° 07′ 14″ N 3° 56′ 35″ W): lugging, jougs, hanging, birching and the branks, or scold's bridle. This last device was a humiliating device worn over the face preventing the offender from speaking. These are sometimes associated with witchcraft, but in Stirling tended to be for perceived 'uppity women' who criticized their social betters.

John Harrison has conducted extensive research into Stirling's branks and has revealed that between 1600 and 1722, some 44 women were punished with the branks and a further 106 were threatened with it. The branks was a very flexible punishment, it could be worn or carried for differing periods of time depending on the 'crime'; you might also have to

The keystone of the Tolbooth arch: mute witness to centuries of judgment

---

[102]   It's important not to fall into the *Outlander* trap: Jamie and the Jacobites were part of a British Civil War and absolutely not resisting a genocidal English invasion run by self-hating sadomasochistic gay rapists!

walk around the city to subject yourself to public pillory and shame.

What I always find astonishing is what people were punished for.[103] It often comes down to simple name-calling and certainly reveals that society was more rigid in the past and that people had to know their place, women especially. However, occasionally even underdogs can be pushed too far. In May 1702 a press gang[104] swept down from the Castle and seized men, who of course were the main breadwinners for families. The leader of the gang, Captain Sharp, pointed a loaded gun at Patrick McFarland, but a woman named Mareon McFarlane grabbed the gun and said he would *'shoot none at that time'*. Other women joined in what became known as the Women's Riot and, for their bravery, all of them ended up in court.

It would be over 150 years until the woman's suffrage movement gained any status and while it was, in general, peaceful there was a strong militant strand and there were three very notable acts of protest. The most famous was in August 1912 when the glass case holding the Wallace Sword (the fake one) was smashed by Ethel Moorhead and a hand-printed note was left inside:

'Your liberties were won by the sword. Release the women who are fighting for their liberties. Stop the forcible feeding.[105] A protest from Dublin.'

Ethel chose to go to Perth jail for seven days.

A year later at the opening ceremony for a statue of former Prime Minister Sir Henry Campbell-Bannerman (see below) by the then-Prime Minister Hugh Asquith, he had his car blocked and pepper thrown into it. Another tried to strike him with a whip. All the women involved were charged. Intriguingly,

---

[103]   Mind you, all of Stirling was shocked in to learn in May 1582 that Robert Cousland was living with one Issobell Olephant, despite being told to put her aside. They were banned from eating or drinking together and from talking to each other. Gosh, no date night then!

[104]   Press gangs were fairly common in the 17th and 18th centuries, and in one particularly bad case in April 1696 a man had been locked up in St Ninians as part of the local quota for recruitment, but a soldier found him and carried him off at gun point, forcing the locals to find a someone else – the quota still had to be met.

[105]   This relates to arrested women who went on hunger strike and were then force fed.

none of these women were from Stirling; they were all from Glasgow or Edin-burgh. The third, a much more sedate protest was more likely undertaken by local women. In September 1913 a bowling green at Bridge of Allan was vandal-ised. Deep cuts were made in the grass to insert slips of paper saying '*Justice for women before bowls*'. Quite right.

One of Stirling's most impressive 17th century buildings is Cowane's Hos-pital (279169, 693679; 56° 07′ 14″ N 3° 56′ 42″ W), the best-preserved late medi-eval hospital in Scotland. Now as you may know, Cowane's Hospital is not an A&E[106] but rather an alms house for looking after members of the Merchant's Guild when they fell on hard times.[107] It also features Scotland's oldest playable bowling green, and its back wall is built to the same specifications as the City Wall.

17th century nails from Cowane's Hospital

It was being repaired and conserved all throughout 2019, and I was lucky enough to get some behind the scenes tours dur-ing the works. The roof was be-ing completely replaced, which means the original slates were taken off and put back up with better nails. This is because the original iron nails had rusted, a process called nail rot, and been removed – so of course the ground was littered with them. Unlike modern nails which are round in profile, these nails were individually made by blacksmiths and have square profiles. Given the cost of transport in the past, these nails were likely made close by in Stirling.

---

[106]   Although it did play a key role in the 1832 cholera epidemic which killed 32 people, while a second outbreak in 1837 killed 100 people in a single week.

[107]   It was clearly an act of penance for a life lived as a sharp-edged business-man. Certainly he sinned, and in 1611 he was fined £6 for fathering an il-legitimate son. A near hagiography of the man, published in 1919, makes no mention of his son and this incident is recorded in the following man-ner: '*his name appears in the [church] records in circumstances not so honourable, but which appear to have been of such frequent occurrence with all classes of the community that the record of them constitutes the greater portion of the Session Minutes*'.

John Harrison has noted that over 28,000 nails were used to build the hospital's roof, including several hundred from John McArthur. St Ninians and Bannockburn were once home to a thriving nail industry, and it's probable that the nails pictured above were made there. The earliest record of a nail maker in the area is William Lockhart, who was making nails for Stirling Castle in 1633. So perhaps the nails above were made by William or John; certainly they are all that remains of a once thriving industry, and are now in the safekeeping of Cowane's Trust.

The object in the picture is the base of a wheel turned pot. Can you see the spiral caused by the potter's fingers? It was made about 1650-1700, probably in Throsk, and was found in 2016 in the grounds of a 17th century mansion in Stirling which was demolished in 1900. The vessel itself was thrown away around 1800.

While these pots are similar in function to the bowls and cups in your kitchen, they definitely look weird. The fabric is grey, not white, as the clay was dug up from around Stirling. The firing was a bit rubbish, so sometimes the pots are a bit wobbly (think about all those gifts you made your parents in pottery classes). The other thing was that all the pots available – unless you had money and could import stuff

The base of a pot from Throsk

from England or the continent – were covered in a green glaze, the easiest colour to mass produce. Imagine how dull meals would have been.

Nobody really thinks about Throsk anymore. It's just another wee place you drive past on the way to somewhere else, or perhaps you've done that cycle along the long flat road. Or maybe you've never even driven that way, travelling east along the bigger roads. But in addition to an extensive pottery industry, Throsk was also one of the most important places in Stirling. The Abbott of Cambuskenneth had a palace there from perhaps the 12th century, which survived to the 17th and 18th centuries, and the current Throsk Farmhouse may be all that's left. So when you pass next, think about all that change, how brief our lives are, and try to have more fun... or in my case, do more digging!

In archaeology, documents change everything. This rather unassuming rickle of stones, which sits high above Sheriffmuir (283918, 702037; 56° 11′ 48″ N

The collapsed remains of James Menteith's House

3° 52′ 21″ W), is actually all that remains of James Menteith's house and it sits in the middle of his former farm, Glentye. While it's on a south-facing slope, it's a good 30 minute hike from the road, over some very rough grazing land – not made any easier to walk through by swearing. At first glance this appears to be completely uneconomic. I never even spotted any sheep, which perhaps explains why it was abandoned around 1800. However, the farm was leased from James Stirling of Keir for £67 a year, and when James Menteith died in 1719 he left a small fortune of £26,500 and was one of the richest men in Dunblane Parish. We only know so much about him as he left a very detailed will.

James was a very successful businessman and owned livestock and land which he rented out; he sold milk and cheese, rented rooms to students at Dunblane burgh school and even sold guns and books on occasion. He traded with people from all over Scotland, all of whom came to Dunblane and Stirling for markets and fairs.

His business took an upturn following the Union of the Parliaments, and indeed it was so successful that his landlord raised the rent. However, The Jacobite Rising of 1715 was a bad year and he virtually stopped trading. The Jacobites burnt six local settlements, all of which resulted in the Battle of Sherrifmuir[108] which covered an enormous area that is now full of objects. Over the years there have been several metal detecting surveys of the battlefield and my favourite find was a shoe buckle found 2km from the front line, presumably caught in a rabbit hole by a fleeing soldier.

There was fear and uncertainty all over the county. Stirling Bridge was guarded by soldiers led by Colonel John Blackadder (his father was the Covenanting Minister and nothing to do with Rowan Atkinson) until the day after

---

[108] Neither the Jacobites nor the Government really won this one but, as it was a Jacobite Rising, technically they lost as they certainly hadn't won!

the battle, as no one was sure who had won. In the city, one John Wright got into trouble for firing a gun at some strangers who were in his boss's yard. Were these Jacobite spies, robbers or simply people out for a walk? The economic impact of the Rising was worse than the conflict, and was felt for two more years. It was even worse for our hero

The arch of Stirling Old Bridge that Blakeney destroyed

James Menteith, as his landlord's estate was confiscated for his role in the Rising and he owed James over £3,000, having borrowed from his very successful business. A salutary lesson on the impact of war and invasion – even if you survive.

As we've heard, some of James' wealth came from the cattle trade and he was not alone: between 1600 and 1889[109] over 100 million head of cattle travelled from the north of Scotland to the markets to the south and most crossed the Forth at Stirling across Stirling Old Bridge (279702, 694572; 56° 07′ 43″ N 3° 56′ 13″ W). So you can imagine the impact its closure caused. But what on earth could shut down Scotland's most important Bridge? Nothing less than a threat to national security. In 1745, ahead of Bonnie Prince Charlie's siege of Stirling Castle (the last ever), the town had surrendered.[110] General Blakeney,[111] who was in charge of the castle,[112] cut the inner arch of the bridge to trap the Jaco-

---

[109] Of course this marked the opening of the Forth Rail Bridge – at the time the biggest bridge in the world.

[110] There was subsequently a rather craven attempt by the Stirling authorities to explain their hasty acquiescence to the Jacobite menace, which basically stated that that as there was no back wall to the city, there was no point in barring the front gate!

[111] While he failed to trap Bonnie Prince Charlie, after Culloden he was promoted and put in charge of the Highlands.

[112] A later Lieutenant Governor of the Castle Lt General Samuel Graham, fought during the American Wars of Independence (for King George). He

bites in Stirling. It didn't work, though; the Jacobites beat a government army at Falkirk and went over the Fords of Frew, accidently blowing up St Ninians on the way (this was where they stored their gunpowder). It's not precisely clear what happened at St Ninians, but it appears that as the Jacobites were gather-ing up the gunpowder, they asked locals to help them and some of them helped themselves, filling their pockets and hiding gunpowder under the church seats. A guard spotted this and fired, igniting the gunpowder and blowing the church up! The local community rebuilt the church, with reused stone, on a different spot a few years later.

The bridge was closed between December 1745 and March 1749. The Council's temporary solution to the bridge closure was to use boats to ferry people, stock and goods across the river and to charge for the journey. Before you splutter your coffee over this book, it's worth noting that the Council had always charged for the use of the bridge, which had gates to control movement. Indeed, in 1710 the Council appointed someone to pursue cattle drovers who used the Fords of Frew,[113] thus avoiding the fee at the bridge.

The bridge also holds a much darker secret. In 1606 Stirling was ravaged by a plague and, in a last desperate move, the city quarantined the dead and the dying on the other side of the bridge. It's estimated that 600 people died during the plague, many of them making their last journey across the bridge. The corpses were taken back over for reburial at a place called The Death Rig (or field), the location of which is now lost.

was at one point camped on Long Island, New York and was attacked by American troops who crossed the ice. General Washington gave orders to draw lots for his life with 12 other British Officers. This was in retaliation for the lynching of an American Captain (Joshua Huddy) by loyalists and only after the British had refused to hand over the perpetrators. Graham survived the ordeal and wrote about in his memoirs!

[113] Yes, the same place Kenneth II fortified, that Bonnie Prince Charlie crossed at and that perhaps William The Conqueror crossed!

Chapter Nine

Stirling, A City of Empire: 1750-1918

A Time of Transformation

Social change and technological advancement

In 1750 the town was more or less the same size as it had been in 1550. Edinburgh and Glasgow boomed: there was trade with the Empire and the Enlightenment, one of the world's greatest intellectual movements. The cash from Empire played a decisive role in securing Scotland's place in the Union. Stirling, however, wallowed in corruption and decay. The infamous Black Bond of 1771 was an agreement between city officials to divvy up positions and income between themselves. This was so bad that in 1773 the Council elections were declared void by the courts, *'having been brought about by undue influence and corrupted practices'*, and the Council was abolished until 1781.

A present from a grateful Empire: Campbell-Bannerman's Statue

     The political corruption was combined with a physical one: a collapsing drainage and water system led to the streets functioning as open sewers; blood from the slaughterhouse in St John's Street simply ran down the hill. Added to this was the old Scots custom of throwing human waste (or night soil) out the window: 'garde loo'. This is famously described in Edinburgh by 18th century poet Robert Fergusson, Burns' inspiration, where the results are described as flowers blooming each morning:

'They kindly shower Edina's roses,
To quicken and regale our noses'

In 1841, one Dr Forrest describes waste from some 60 or so prisoners in the jail, floating all the way to King Street as regular as clockwork with the daily slopping out, which created '*The most offensive and disgusting odour*'. Of course, this fed into the water supply which was already wholly inadequate. There are 18th century descriptions of people queuing for several hours to get water for the day, and one person counted over 200 pails and buckets waiting to be filled.

The upshot was of course disease, misery and death. We have covered the plague of 1606 and the cholera epidemics of 1832 and 1837, where Dr Forrest was again a heroic key player. There are also accounts of guards being stationed at gates to deter strangers, and at the end of the 19th century Stirling had the lowest life expectancy and highest infant mortality in Scotland. Of course all of this was aided by the flight of the middle classes from the old town to newer developments to the north (Bridge Street) and south (Allan Park) of the city. What was left, the dens and wynds of the Top o' The Town, became a core of disease, poverty and crime. Its subsequent demolition in the 1940s and 1960s was an attempt to end this cycle.

Eventually, by 1848, a clean water supply was established from a new reservoir near Touch above Cambusbarron. The campaigning efforts of Dr Forrest were again instrumental. However, not all doctors were such good eggs, and famously another Dr Forrest (the good doctor's second cousin) was interested in illegally obtaining fresh corpses for dissection practice. He bribed the local gravedigger James McNab and his pal Daniel Mitchel to steal the corpse of newly-buried Mary Stevinson. The disturbed grave was discovered and a riot ensued, but Forrest fled before he could be arrested. Sometime later there was a rumour that the more famous Edinburgh graverobber William Burke – of Burke and Hare fame – had moved in to St Mary's Wynd. After a frantic house to house search revealed no trace of the miscreant, things calmed down.

However, throughout the same period there was also change and expansion. After 1745 Scotland had peace, and slowly but surely even Stirling began to enjoy the fruits of both Empire and the industrial revolution. This had a series of enormous impacts on the city and wider region, which were transformed almost beyond recognition as wealth was clawed from the ground.

The biggest of these changes were to the bogs east and west of Stirling and their transformation into fertile farmland. This work had been going on for centuries,[114] but it rapidly scaled up in the 18th century through the actions of

dozens of small lease holders, derogatorily called Moss Lairds.[115] They were offered 38 year leases and given timber to build a house and enough oatmeal for a year. They paid no rent for the first seven years, after which rent slowly rose over time. One of main landowners was the judge Lord Kames of Blair Drummond, who was also a leading figure of Edinburgh's Enlightenment. He confirmed that slavery was illegal in Scotland 1777 and supported one of my heroes, David Hume.[116] Kames and his son heavily invested in the process and cut a three-mile channel right across the Carse from Blair Drummond to the Forth. The water was drained by an enormous water wheel, The Great Mill of Torr, which was demolished in 1870. The Kames' seem to

The Kames Memorial (272475, 698668; 56° 09 ' 49" N 4° 03 ' 18" W)

have cleared around 1,500 acres of peat in their time.

Once the land had been cleared of peat, it was still too acidic to grow crops and so lime had to be spread across it. Lime had been quarried and burnt (to turn it to quicklime) for centuries from the upper stretches of the Bannock-

---

[114]   There is a charter from 1314 to Robert The Bruce confirming the right to the Burgesses of Stirling to cut peat at Skeoch, which lies near the Bannockburn. This is also the location of one of Stirling's earliest coal mines.

[115]   I know the great-great grandchildren of quite a few of them!

[116]   As a confirmed atheist, Hume was denied promotion. On his death-bed Samuel Johnson's biographer, Robert Boswell, wanted to know if Hume would recant and ask for the Lord's mercy. Hume did not, and died affirming his beliefs. Whatever your view of faith, Hume was truly a brave man.

An 18ᵗʰ century limekiln at Fallin

burn (remember the fossil beds at Swallowhaugh from earlier?), though traditional methods were no longer enough to meet demand. Vast quantities of limestone was transported, often by boats, and burnt on the land it was to fertilise. Now, burning limestone is a nasty, horrible business; the resultant material is anhydrous and will chemically react with the water in anything organic – the dust would literally blind you.

Whatever the human cost, it worked. A survey in 1811 confirmed that the cleared land at Blair Drummond was home to 764 men, women and children along with 264 cows, 166 horses, 375 hens, 30 pigs, 168 cats, and eight dogs. This was another part of the aforementioned agricultural revolution in Scotland. However, I suspect we might now rather have the complete bog with all its biodiversity and safely stored carbon.

Other new industries included coal mining and glass works which provided hundreds if not thousands of new jobs. Iron working was still a strong employer and 1,000 nails a day were made by 113 people in four mills at St Ninians. Further afield, the Carron Iron Works was established in Falkirk in 1759 and became a massive weapons complex[117] as well as a household name. Rather disappointingly, while there are six cannons in Stirling,[118] none were made by The Carron Iron Works. However, they did make

A witch's cauldron from Carron Iron Works

---

[117] Carronades, named after the plant, were a revolutionary short range cannon used from the 1770s to the Boer War. They gave the British a tactical advantage in 18ᵗʰ century naval battles and were used by the HMS *Victory* at the Battle of Trafalgar.

[118] The two at Cowane's Hospital were captured from the Russian Tsar during the Crimean Campaign and have the imperial double eagle on them.

The view from The Butt Well to Ben Lomond

cauldrons like the one pictured which belongs to my colleague Fiona Buchanan's mother. Now these are found all over the world, and were so ubiquitous that in America they became the go-to spooky old cauldron – obviously used by witches.

All of these businesses brought ever more money into Stirling, and there were a series of improvements as a result. The very pleasant Back Walk was formalised in the late 18th century and there followed planting schemes, extensions and benches in the 19th century – there was even a 'keeper of the walk' from 1817 to 1860. Eventually, the path stretched from the Barras Yett[119] (the city gate) to Gowan Hill and the Beheading Stone, and even in the late 18th century it was described by the local minister as '*perhaps the finest thing of its kind that any place can boast of*'. It was clearly a great source of pride; there was, however, a wee problem. In the general improvements made around the town, the open sewers from the castle – which once emptied onto Ballengeich Road (over James V's wee path, which was by now very slippy) – had been moved to the south side, where they were supposed to run into cess pits which would be emptied and used as fertiliser on King's Park Farm. However, such was the

---

[119]   This was where Wallace's arm was supposed to have been placed, though it was more likely on Stirling Bridge. And just outside this location was where Stirling's medieval lepers were based, as they were banned from the city.

smell that the workers refused, and the charming aroma remained to enhance the genteel walk around the castle. Elsewhere, transport links were improved. The remaining gate on Stirling Bridge was removed, as was the medieval Barras Yett which had once been flung open to welcome Bonnie Prince Charlie.

Towards the end of the 18th century, following the French Revolutionary Wars, Napoleon came to power and there was a 12 year worldwide clash between Britain and France for dominancy. The carronades helped at sea and, on land, the British Army became ever more organised and professional. There were a series of consequences for all of Scotland, but there were a number of specific impacts on Stirling. The first was that because tourism to Europe was blocked, interest turned northwards – Scotland and The Lake District were rediscovered. Now, the Scotland that people discovered was chiefly created by Sir Walter Scott. His blockbuster poem *The Lady of The Lake* wove Scottish history and myth with Arthurian legend and real locations, including the aforementioned Trossachs and Mote Hill. He helped promote tartan, rediscovered Scotland's Crown Jewels and managed the first visit of a British monarch to Scotland for over 150 years. The stereotypical biscuit tin image of stags and tartan has its roots in Scott.

The growth of the Empire and the success against Napoleon all had impacts on Scotland and Stirling. We were drawn ever closer into partnership with England, Stirling became more clearly a garrison town,[120] and in 1807 a brand new parade ground was built outside the castle[121] (the current car park) with steps to the ever-improving Back Walk. In 1881 the Argyll and Sutherland Highlanders were formed from two earlier regiments (93rd Sutherland Highlanders and the 91st (Princess Louise's Argyllshire) Regiment), and Stirling became their base.[122] In turn, this created a series of clear and distinct sets of consequences: money, fame and military careers could be made in the glorious service of the Empire. Some of these 'glorious' campaigns included the conquest of

---

[120]   Though to be fair it had had a regular garrison since about the 1640s.

[121]   Ownership is still disputed with the Council, who claim it was only loaned!

[122]   Famously, this regiment had the largest cap badge in the British army, which features a red and white check commemorating the Thin Red Line, which was formed by the 93rd to break the Russian cavalry charge at Balaklava during the Crimean Campaign – the first time this had ever happened. And of course, this is the campaign that those cannons at Cowanes came from.

southern Africa and the repression of the Indian Mutiny (or the First War of Indian Independence), where a fairly routine punishment for the rebelling troops was for them to be tied to loaded cannons, which were then fired.

It is sometimes hard to find the detail of these lives from so long ago, but the internet makes it is so much easier. After some years of gentle if persistent persuasion from my daughters and friends, I finally got a smartphone and I must say it is indeed very smart. It has completely transformed the walks I take around Stirling, it's easier to photograph things and incredibly easy to research them. Which, of course, means they were right all along. (Don't tell them, though!)

Anyway, the monument pictured is in the Old Town Cemetery. It's a classic early 19th century obelisk which commemorates members of the Baird family, two of whom were in the military: Lieutenant Colonel James Baird and Major Patrick Baird. A quick internet search on my new phone revealed that these two were brothers and that both had fought with Wellington against Napoleon, which is pretty cool in and of itself. However, they were also nephews of the more famous Colonel Sir David Baird.

David Baird was a typical 19th century hero; he fought in India, Egypt and Portugal against Napoleon and his allies. He features in a very famous painting by David Wilkie regarding the discovery of Tipu Sultan's body (now revered as a leader of India's resistance to British rule), and is even in the Sharpe novels. Famously, he was severely wounded in India and held for four years in chains with a festering bullet that was not removed from him un-

Wellington's Men: The Baird Memorial

til he was released. Upon hearing that he was in chains, his mother famously said, '*God help the chiel chained to our Davie*'.

Anyway, a much more tenuous link, but one which still demonstrates the mobility of the Scottish middle classes across the Empire's structure, is the story of General Sir John Moore, the hero of the Battle of Corunna who was fatally wounded there[123] and who has a famous University in Liverpool named after him. His father was born in the now-demolished manse of Holy Rude Church.

Elsewhere, the money from Empire and The East India Company flooded into Scotland, and brand new estates were built at Plean and Aithrey.[124] These people had so much money that they could move entire villages and public roads. Of the two original villages to either side of Aithrey, both were reduced to single houses. However, these were not the Highland Clearances; the houses were dilapidated, and people were very pleased to be moved into nice new houses closer to town.

Robert Burns: Scotland's National Bard

With the success of the Napoleonic Campaigns and the growth of internal tourism, attention turned to Scotland's history and battlefields, and Bannockburn was of course a key focus. Burns had already celebrated it with his wonderful *Scots Wa Hae* and Scott had his new house at Abbotsford to pay for, so he churned out another epic poem, *The Lord of the Isles,* which culminates in the Battle of Bannockburn. Scott's poems celebrate a particular vision of a noble heroic past and derring-do – something Mark Twain criticised Scott for, decrying his checking of '*this wave of progress... (and setting) the world in love with dreams and phantoms; with decayed and swinish forms of religion; with decayed and degraded systems of government; with the silliness and emptiness, sham grandeurs, sham gauds, and sham chivalries of a brainless and worthless long-vanished society.*' (Hey, that's Scotland, he's talking about! Albeit Scott's particular version of it.[125])

---

123   Wives accompanied officers on this campaign and the coach of Mrs MacKenzie, the aunt of a leading member of Stirling's high society, came under fire from the French and was heard to remark '*Will no one shut that hole and keep the wind out?* Apparently Uncle MacKenzie was standing next to Sir John Moore when he was shot.

124   Where St Serf had been performing miracles over a 1000 years before!

125   Scott has definitely fallen out of fashion, but his best stuff really is very good and worth persevering with.

● ● ●

This celebration of our military past culminated with the construction of the National Wallace Monument, the largest monument to an individual in Britain, completed in 1869. This of course raises the question as to why Scotland felt it necessary to erect the largest constructed monument to Scottish independence? Yes, there was certainly concern about a loss of Scottish identity,[126] but there was no serious suggestion of independence (yet) – although there had always been passionate individuals proposing everything from Home Rule to full independence, and Stirling would host the ratification of the Scottish National Party in 1928. I think a clue lies in the song that won the competition to be sung at the banquet to commemorate the laying of the foundation stone of the Wallace Monument in 1861: *The Battle of Stirling Bridge* by William Sinclair. Apparently it was very famous, though unfortunately almost completely forgotten today.[127] The conclusion of the song stresses that despite being at war with each other, Scotland, England and Ireland are now at peace:

The shamrock, rose, the thistle stern,
Shall wave around her Wallace cairn,
And bless the brave for ever.

The same sentiment is better expressed by Charles McKay, who described:

and though no longer foes;
are the Thistle and the Rose,
but in love intertwined,
and with Erin's Shamrock joined-
In prosperity, in valour and in worth.

To be explicit and to slightly editorialise: for the best part of a 1000 years Scotland and England were at war with each other, and as soon as we were at peace we took over the world. For some reason the Welsh were excluded from

---

[126] Like many places in Scotland there was a riot in Stirling in 1706 when the Articles of The Treaty of Union were publicly burnt. The military recorded the names of those involved and reported them to the higher authorities – quite what was done with this intelligence is unknown!

[127] It, along with lots of others, features in Victorian anthology of poetry about Stirling *The Harp of Stirlingshire...* well worth tracking down, if you can find it!

this glorious poetic vision, although the leek was considered a suitable decorative motif and often appears with the thistle rose and shamrock.

Now there was of course a much darker side to all of this, and I'm not simply talking about the Empire which of course was built from conquered countries whose shores were invaded, whose populations were killed and whose wealth was taxed.[128] I'm also not really talking about the problems that emerge in garrison towns, though they were were rife.[129] Soldiers bullied local traders: for example John Lyon, a shoemaker who hadn't repaired Sergeant William Pollock's shoes quick enough. Pollock arrived at Lyon's house brandishing a sword, a hand grenade and a lit match – all to encourage progress. To make matters worse, the soldiers often reneged on their bills before being posted elsewhere. Other problems included local women mixing with soldiers

Partners in Empire: the thistle, rose, leek and shamrock

who tended – on a regular basis – to get moved on and abandon their responsibilities, leaving single mothers with few if any choices.[130] Still yet more problems were associated with injured veterans who hung about the city without any formal systems of support, or who were simply demobbed without any money. There was even a riot in December 1697,[131] when a group of disbanded soldiers

[128] I appreciate that some good came from the Empire, and that of course Britain sacrificed its world power status in the defeat of the Nazis, but I would prefer to leave final judgment to those who were conquered.

[129] The Stirling garrison presented a particularly unique and Scottish problem: many of them were from the Highland (which started a mere 10-20 miles north and west) and were monoglot Gaelic speakers, and so needed translators to be understood in the town!

[130] In the second half of the 18th century Stirling compiled a 'vagabond' book which lists various miscreants, including numerous single mothers. Indeed, in 1711 the Council required local women to report their 'uncleanness' with a soldier before he left the area on pain of public humiliation and banishment.

[131] And is it any wonder? Can you imagine being made redundant with nothing just before Christmas? That is really low.

demanded two weeks' subsistence, refused to put down their arms and fired on their officers.

No, I am talking about child labour and slavery. Of the workforce in the newly expanded late 18th century mining industry, it is estimated that roughly a quarter of the workers were children under the age of 7.[132] In 1832, ten year old William Carr was interviewed at Smith's Woollen Mill in Cowane Street. William reported that he '*got sleepy in the evening and my feet get sore. Sometimes I have a cough, but I like the work well enough. I receive ten shillings a month*[133] *which I give to my mother but she allows me two pence or so. I have never been to school since I started work. None of the young ones go to school. I cannot write*'. We also have figures for the nail trade, in which children as young as seven or eight worked from 6am to 10 or 11pm and were expected to produce up to 1,250 nails a day. Things seem to have been far worse down the mines. In 1842, 12 year old John Allan had worked the pits at Plean from the age of 10; he worked 12-13 hours a day, struggling through flooded tunnels which reached over his knees.

I fully intend to come back to the mining industry, but there is a more pressing and squalid evil that also helped fund Stirling's beautiful streets: slavery. As we have heard, the practice has unfortunately left scars across our city's entire history. There are records of Roman slaves making salt on the Forth, their owners patrolling the Antonine Wall. In the early 12th century we learn that St Ninians Kirk was granted, in perpetuity, the lives of the slaves that worked its land. It's likely that the Wars of Independence broke up the social order and slavery vanished from Scotland soon after. But of course it raised its ugly head again in the 18th century and, while you could not be enslaved in Scotland, you could perhaps be bought elsewhere and brought here. The courts eventually stopped this nonsense, and in 1834 slavery was banned across the British Empire.

If you're from Stirling, you may have heard one or several rumours about the Black Boy on top of our most famous fountain. I see this fountain a few times a day, as it's on my way to work. It sits just outside the medieval city. It was the site of the gallows and it holds a secret: it's not a memorial to the Black

---

132   While throughout the 19th century there were various reforms, work for under 14 year olds was only banned in the 1930s. My own father started work at 15 in the 1960s.

133   The average wage for a trained artisan was two shillings and sixpence a day.

Death or African slavery (both local stories are made up), nor is it true that at one point it was covered in clothing so as not to upset any sensitive souls due to its naked state (a joke, and not the actions of prurient Victorian Councillors!). The wee boy at the top is a cherub and it's originally from Glasgow, having been built to celebrate a visit from Queen Victoria in 1849. We got it on the cheap afterwards.

The Black Boy Fountain: not a monument commemorating the horrors of slavery, though perhaps it should be

However, slave owners were compensated when slavery was banned and those records are listed in an excellent website run by University College London called *Legacy of British Slave-ownership*. This website mundanely and precisely lists the well-heeled streets all around The Black Boy Fountain, a blood-curdling account of evil: lives as pounds, shilling and pence, with 9 Stirling residents owning 1640 men, women and children. I think about them every time I walk past.

For nearly 200 years, mining was one of Scotland's main industries and it has left the scars of pits and bings all over the landscape.[134] Of course, there was a huge demand for coal for industrial and domestic purposes. The wee red door shown below is one of dozens all through the lovely lanes of King's Park. It doesn't have a handle, can only be opened from the inside and is at shoulder height. It's an echo of an older technology, one that most would say is archaic, irresponsible and dangerous – and only the middle and upper classes had one. So what exactly is it?

A coal bunker in King's Park

It's a door to a coal bunker, for the fire. Have a look up at all those chimneys and think just how much we burned. If you lived in King's Park, you certainly didn't want a mucky coal man trudging up your stairs and getting your carpet filthy. For those that lived in The Top o' The Town, there was no choice: the coal sat next to the fire, perhaps in a bunker under the window. At least

---

[134]   One of the largest is over the Day Two Bannockburn battlefield.

that way they didn't have to hump the coal themselves. Although of course neither did the denizens of King's Park – they had servants.

Younger readers may not realise how much we relied on coal and how horrible it was, going out in the rain to fill the coal skuttle (that was my job), waking up to a cold house and having to kindle the fire to heat the water to wash (again, my job), the coal dust on the walls that had to be washed before they could be painted and the thousands and thousands of men, women and children underground, suffering in close, confining claustrophobia.

If that were not bad enough, our social betters did not even want to see the men walking to the pits and miners were banned from taking a short cut through the King's Park (now the golf course) in their working clothes, in case it lowered the tone! Like many of you, I had family that went down the pits –

and this makes my blood boil.

I don't mourn the end of mining. Even ignoring the carbon footprint, it was a nasty industry. My grandad rarely talked about it, but he had nightmares about being trapped underground in the dark. Sometimes the mines took more than a good night's sleep. At the side of the road in Plean is this small, discreet and understated monument dedicated to the 12 men and boys (look at the ages) who died in East Plean Pit on the 13th July 1922, in an explosion a mile underground.

The cost of coal: The Plean Memorial

The memorial, however, reveals nothing of the details, all of which were chillingly recorded afterwards in interviews with the survivors. Mr Frank McCann's always sticks in my head; he was with his son Bernard, who was 30: '*I... immediately picked up my light and shouted up to the two boys that it was gas. We had only 100 feet to go to reach the level road, but on getting about half way we were knocked down in the dark... we had a terrible struggle to get into the level road and after that I could not tell any more. It was an awful explosion. I don't understand why my son Bernard did not escape. I lost him at the foot of the heading... No one has any idea of what it is unless he has come through it'.* Can there be any more poignant example of survivor's guilt and pain? Groping blind and panicking in the choking dark for the son you would never hold again. And can you imagine having to return to work, to the thing that took your son and nearly claimed you? There was a brave man.

The second half of the 19th century saw a massive growth, and Stirling doubled and then tripled in size. The railway came in 1848,[135] and wealthy merchants from Glasgow wanted somewhere with clean air and brilliant views so Stirling became a commuting town with the construction of King's Park. At the same time, there was industrial expansion down towards the Forth.

Returning to King's Park: have you ever wandered round it? Have you ever looked at the wee low walls that define the front gardens? They are now all a bit squat and ugly, but they shouldn't be; they were built when Stirling (or at least King's Park) was amongst the richest places in the world, and the owners

Wealth from Empire: King's Park decorative metal work

wanted people to know and be impressed with how fashionable they were. Scotland led the world in cast iron, and our decorative metalwork is still found all over the place. This, of course, was where local firm James Davie and Sons made their money, and you can still see their wonderful cast iron framework in the train station.

The railings and decorative iron work still survives in odd places around town, where there was a steep drop or on roof lines or weather vanes. But you have to pay attention to find it, so take your time and look up (but not when crossing the road). They're absolutely brilliant; look at the detail: public sculpture of the very best.

But where did it all go? Well, in World War II there was a perceived shortage of iron for the war effort and it was volunteered by the public to help beat the Nazis. However, apparently too much was gathered (over a millions tons across the UK by September 1944), and much of it was simply left to rust in Council Depots.

In addition to the metal work, there were also ornate stone carvings, most of which drew on Stirling and Scotland's past. On those grand Victorian and Edwardian buildings that survived the 1960s and 1970s, I have counted 125

---

135   The first station was a simple wooden hut which led to numerous complaints from those commuting to Glasgow and Edinburgh. Readers will be pleased to learn that the great-great-great grandchildren of those commuters still find plenty to moan about regarding the train to this day.

More showing off: Some Stirling Victorian carved heads

heads comprising 40 lions and big cats, 21 portraits, 16 dragons, 15 Greek Gods, 11 gargoyles, five foxes, four satyrs, two each of Wallaces, Scotts and Burns, two eagles, one Bruce, one Queen Victoria, a Green Man (more about him and his brethren below), a bat and an owl.

The same increase in wealth can be seen across the Victorian graves in Stirling's cemeteries, which get bigger, more elaborate and contain more information. So it's much easier to research people – as we heard earlier with the Baird family. Personally, I prefer the older ones; they're more interesting as works of art and here are my three favourites:

Green Men are characterised by having foliage for hair and tendrils coming from their mouth. They are pre-Christian fertility symbols, and were adopted in the medieval period as gargoyles. They reappear in the 17th and 18th century and seem to reflect masons wanting to do something different and have fun. What makes these later ones even odder is that there is always a cherub on the other side, perhaps reflecting some kind of duality.

Pagan and Christian

● ● ●

I thought this one was decidedly pagan. It's a snake eating its own tail: the ouroboros. It's a symbol for infinity and first appears in ancient Egypt. In a Christian context it reflects the Alpha and the Omega of the Greek Alphabet, the cycle of birth and rebirth and ultimately Christ's promise of eternal life.

A very hungry snake: an ouroboros

Now for me this is perhaps the most pagan of the lot of them. It's a pelican, but it's also a symbol of Christ and the Eucharist: this reflects Christ's Last Supper, when he encouraged the disciples to break bread and drink wine to consume his body and blood. The reason the Pelican is featured is because, according to legend, they are supposed to feed their young from their own flesh.

A symbol of sacrifice: pelicans

Now, as you may realise, I love wandering the Old Town Cemetery and so I know Tam Rennie (an all-round good egg), who helps manage the gravediggers. We were talking about our favourite stones, and Tam showed me his... and here it is.

A Gaelic bone setter: Daniel Ferguson

Daniel Ferguson was a bone-setter, and this monument was erected by his grateful patients. Just in case you didn't know what a bone-setter was, there's a cool depiction of a broken bone at the top. So yes, before you ask, he mended broken bones and ensured that they healed in the correct way. Now Daniel was a traditional healer with roots in the medieval Gaelic tradition.[136] Before the NHS, doctors were expensive and, in a manual labouring economy with poor health and safety, physical injuries

---

[136] It's entirely possible that Daniel might have been denounced as a witch in the 17th century.

were common. If that were not enough, there is that wonderful bronze profile sculpture of him – and if you peer at it close enough, you will find that it was made by a Daniel Ferguson from Glasgow, who in his time was a reasonably famous sculptor producing images for gravestones and even did the railings for his ancestor Rob Roy's grave at Balquidder. And no, those names are not a coincidence: the bone-setter was the uncle of the sculptor. However, this appears to have been his only commission in Stirling. So why not head up there and see if you can spot it?

Mary, Queen of Scots

One of Stirling's most elaborate buildings is the former Council HQ and, for me, more than any other in Stirling, it so very eloquently depicts the city's changing status. It was built at the peak of Empire, and it celebrates Bruce, Wallace, and Mary, Queen of Scots.[137] Its richly decorated interior continues the theme with stained glass celebrating the foundation of the burgh in 1124 and its pride in the Argyll and Sutherlands (not surprising, as it was completed in 1918). A proposed northern wing was never added, as the money ran out. In the middle of the 20th century, during the demolition of the medieval old town (more of that later on), a new wing was added in a near-brutalist form of architecture with the neighbouring, newly-built tax office (now a Weth-

Out with the old: the burgh seal over time

---

[137]   The first ever statue of her in Scotland.

erspoon's pub) forming a gateway to a modern bright future for Stirling. Both are rather dull and ugly in my opinion – but make your own mind up.

Now, in this rush to modernity, the burgh – the legal foundation of the city for over 800 years – was abolished. The Provost was replaced by a Convenor and, at the same time, God appeared to have been cast aside too. Two versions of Stirling's Burgh seal are shown above. The one on the left is the traditional version while the one on the right is from the front of the right wing of the Municipal Buildings (279537, 693442; 56° 07′ 07″ N 3° 56′ 21″ W). You will see that Christ on the cross has been replaced by an arrow slit on a generic castle. You may of course view this as entirely appropriate – and that is up to you.

Perhaps the grandest interior in Stirling is the magnificent 1915 station (which replaced the wooden hut) with its curving and arcing cast iron framework, designed by James Miller,[138] which has an A-Listed status. Now this was made by a local firm: James Davie and Sons. Their foundry sat proudly amongst the eastern expansion of the city, which breeched the city walls.

There is almost nothing left of the medieval city around this area, as the both the Victorian and the subsequent 1970s re-development were incredibly extensive. We lost mills, the Town Burn Lade and the Town Mill Pond. But the one proud, lone survivor is a City Wall Bastion (one of only two). This

stands incongruously in the midst of a shopping centre car park. It has one gun loup designed to protect the eastern gate, but which now points to a brick wall.

But back to James Davie. Normally when I walk round Stirling I'm looking up at either the wonderful skyline or the magnificent buildings, but after the flash flooding in early 2019,[139] I started looking at the drains and

Stirling's last line of defence: the gun loup in The Thieves Pot

---

138   James lived in Randolphfield House which has two standing stones in its front garden. Tradition links these stones to a skirmish on Day One of the Battle of Bannockburn between Thomas Randolph Early of Moray and Sir Robert Clifford. Of course, I scoffed at this 'myth' - they were more likely to be prehistoric, I thought. So I dug the foundation of one of them and got a date contemporary with the battle!

139   These were so bad that eight foot deep underpasses filled up and people swam in them!

thinking about all that water. As you know Stirling was once surrounded by an inland sea, and for centuries the land has been soft and boggy which is why there was never any large formal wall around Stirling's north side, as no army could ever attack from that way.

That's when I noticed that some of the drain covers (or stanks) were from Stirling and made by James Davie and Sons. But who was James Davie? The Davie family had been in the iron business since at least 1860. James served his apprenticeship across Glasgow, Hull and Manchester before returning to Stirling and joining his father in 1873 with his son eventually joining him in 1902.

Stirling's Foundry: James Davie and Sons

The business had a reputation for structural castings, and their most famous structures locally were Hayford Mills, the Stirling Arcade and, most magnificent of all, the aforementioned Stirling train station canopy. They also produced castings for Greenock Theatre, Carlisle race course, the Clydebank Singer's Sewing Machine factory, Templeton's Carpet Factory at Glasgow and many more. The stanks and manhole covers were produced in the 1950s and 1960s and appear across Stirling and Perth. Unfortunately, the Goosecroft Road foundry was demolished in 1971 and the Cornton one ceased trading a little later – but at least we still have their wonderful drain covers.[140]

One of the most interesting aspects of the Late Victorian period was just how connected the world was. I recently wandered round St Ninians new cemetery (279644, 691719; 56° 06′ 11″ N 3° 56′ 12″ W), the one around the current church, which as we've heard was built from the remains of the one blown up by Bonnie Prince Charlie.

No one ever really seems to visit this cemetery though it's very peaceful and well worth a visit. Within a very elaborate cast iron enclosure I spotted the pictured memorial. But who exactly was Arthur Herbert Drummond Ramsay-Steel-Maitland? Well, it transpires that he was an MP for Birmingham, first chair of the Conservative Party and occasional Minister, including a turn as the

---

140   There are still Davies in the town, and all are very proud of their family's contribution to Stirling.

**Arthur Herbert Drummond
Ramsay-Steel-Maitland**

wonderfully named Under-Secretary of State for the Colonies. His connection to Stirling was his wife Mary, who was the daughter of someone else with a long triple barreled name: Sir James Ramsay-Gibson-Maitland, 4th Baronet of Barnton and Sauchie (try saying that after three pints).

Now, Sir James was a true pioneer and a very interesting chap. He was behind the Howietoun Fishery, opened in 1873, which was developed to prove that trout could be raised like any other farm animal. His experiments were incredibly successful, although at one point an earlier site flooded, the fish escaped and had to be rounded up. Sir James won a series of awards, including two gold medals in 1883 and 1885 at the International Fisheries Exhibition in Edinburgh. Perhaps his key achievement was to develop a method for the successful transport of large quantities of live fish eggs, which was so effective that they could be sent all the way to New Zealand. Indeed, such was his reputation he was known as the Father of Aquaculture – and given how important this science is going to be in feeding future generations, it's incredible to know that its modern origins lie just up the road.

Now, for people to be connected you have to know both where they are and where you are, and the middle of the 19th century marked the creation of the first accurate map of Scotland. I spotted this strange hieroglyph the last time I was at the MacRae Monument on the Sheriffmuir battlefield. It had been carved on a dyke, which had collapsed and was then uncovered during parking improvements. But what exactly is it? Does it point to lost Jacobite treasure (the 1715 was funded from silver from the Ochils)? Or perhaps to some secret Masonic Society?[141]

A mysterious mark

---

[141]   Incidentally, the origins of Freemasonry are often linked to tiny wee Kippen, where James VI's Master of Works William Schaw was born in

The truth is more mundane. It is an Ordnance Survey benchmark dating from around 1850, one of around 500,000 such marks from across the UK which were used to ensure that survey equipment could be repositioned and an accurate known height recorded.

But they are now defunct. Some have been knocked down or demolished and yet, regardless, even the untouched ones are essentially out of service – for they have all moved. They, like you, are still bouncing back from all those vanished glaciers. The Ordnance Survey itself was originally a military organisation designed to make maps and, in a Scottish context, to make invasion and control easier should there ever have been another Jacobite Rising. Indeed, the first comprehensive map of Scotland, General Roy's Great Map, was started in 1747, a year after Bonnie Prince Charlie was defeated at Culloden.

After the Jacobite cause was lost there was a great scrambling of people to proclaim their allegiance to the Hanoverian State, as the estates of prominent Jacobites like Bannockburn House were forfeited. At Killearn, the laird designed a Union Jack garden to let everyone know what side he was on. The garden is now lost, but Roy's map records his allegiance for ever.[142]

From Stirling to Gallipoli

While I've never found any treasure, I really enjoy metal detection and people are always asking me where they can metal detect. Unfortunately, unlike the Right to Roam, there is no right to metal detect – you always need the landowner's permission, and sometimes the state's. Additionally, whatever you find must be reported to the authorities.

The objects in the picture were found during metal detection at a recent phase of path upgrade in King's Park, just next to the golf course. But what are they? Believe it or not, these are buttons and fixtures and fittings from canvas tents from World War I, when the park was used as a camp and training ground for around 4,000 troops –

Lives lost in the trenches

---

around 1550. He was first a royal clock keeper before being promoted. He is linked to the first formal Masonic Lodge in the late 16th century.

[142]   I was unable to get permission to reproduce this map, but it's freely available from the Scottish National Map Library's web site!

their zig-zag practice trenches are still visible from the air. The fittings are presumably bits of old tents that were simply dumped after the end of the war.

Elsewhere across Stirling, the military took over almost every spare space. The Smith Museum became a stable, big houses became hospitals and even Hayford Mills (277554, 692820; 56° 06′ 45″ N 3° 58′ 14″ W) was taken over for troops. The troops at Hayford Mills were destined to fight at Gallipoli alongside the Anzacs, but their train was derailed at Quintinshill in what is still the worst train disaster in British history, resulting in the loss of over 200 people. Famously the sea landings at Gallipoli, part of the Dardanelles Campaign in Turkey, were a total disaster (over 160,000 British troops died). The campaign had been masterminded by Churchill, who was demoted after the debacle and said to a friend '*I am finished*' – he then resigned from Government and volunteered to fight on the front. As an aside, the organiser of the disastrous sea landings, General Sir Ian Hamilton, is buried just outside Doune at Kilmadock (271674, 700687; 56° 10′ 53″ N 4° 04′ 08″ W).[143]

Stirling's Best Kept Secret...

The British often regard World War II as a key moment in our nation's history, although we were not as key a player as we imagine.[144] The Americans did most of the fighting while the Russians did most of the dying. But I am confident that the Nazis were one of the most evil forces in history, and that their defeat is something for the British and all of the allies to be proud of. A key moment at the start of this defeat was of course D-Day, the largest amphibious invasion ever, involving over 5,000 ships and 175,000 troops from 15 different nations.

Of course, such an incredible event needed a lot of planning. Stirling played two key roles in the preparations: the first and most famous is the Atlantic Wall replica on Sheriffmuir (283790,

Live fire training at the Atlantic Wall replica

---

143   Another wee World War I diversion was the career of Major Crum from Blairlogie, who was a former Chief Scout and was the main proponent of sniping in the trenches in World War I.

144   Let's also not forget the enormous contribution of the Commonwealth Allies.

703670; 56° 12′ 41″ N 3° 52′ 31″ W), which I've written about elsewhere, but it's worth repeating. Expecting invasion, Hitler ordered the construction of a massive series of defences along Europe's coastline, often using slave labour. The key element of these defences was the infamous Atlantic Wall, designed to repel tanks. These were constructed from reinforced concrete, which the Germans excelled in making. Using plans smuggled out of occupied Europe in a biscuit tin, replicas of the wall were built across Britain and the biggest and best preserved one is to the north of Dunblane in what was a top secret research and training ground – the end of the Nazis started here.[145] This was used to both work out how to blow the wall up and also to train troops for the invasion using live fire training.[146]

Smoke and Mirrors: Operation Fortitude North

Now as you remember from Gallipoli and indeed Bannockburn and Stirling Bridge – if you know where the attack is coming from you can prepare for it and if there is a pinch point, even better, as an amphibious invasion through a reinforced concrete wall clearly provides an enormous pinch point. So what you have to do is to create confusion as to where you are going to land and try and split the defending troops. This is where Operation Fortitude North came in. It was a smaller element of a larger plan to spread confusion as to where D-Day would actually take place. A combination of double agents, fake announcements and infrastructure indicated up to 13 different possibilities all across Europe. Fortitude North concerned a fake invasion of Norway. Edinburgh, Dundee and Stirling were the bases of fake troops. According to a double agent nicknamed *Garbo* – a Spanish man named Juan Pujol Garcia – Stirling was the base of the British II Corps. This was confirmed by a second double agent *Brutus*, a Pole named Roman Czerniawski. Fake tanks were constructed around North Third and from March 22nd 1944, fake radio traffic between the fictitious units was coordinated by Colonel R. M. McLeod. In addition, both President Eisenhower and the exiled Norwegian King Haakon VII made speeches asking the Norwegian resistance not to act too soon. The trick worked, and 12 German divisions – perhaps over 100,000 men – remained in Norway.

---

[145] First coined by the wonderful Professor Tony Pollard – cheque's in the post Tony!

[146] Rather strangely, those who trained here do not seem to have taken part in the actual D-Day landings.

Now, in addition to creating fake troops and installations, real assets were hidden. The World War I munitions base at Bandeath (285108, 692436; 56° 06′ 39″ N 3° 50′ 57″ W) was removed from all official maps to prevent it being bombed. While the base was formally decommissioned in 1978, there is a rumour that some of the munitions stored there eventually played a role in the Falklands War and may have

The World War I crane at Bandeath

even sunk the *Belgrano*. The evidence for this was supposedly some graffiti or a sign on one of the stores, but I have not seen it myself. Now, the *Belgrano* was sunk by a Mark VIII Mod 4 torpedo, which were designed in 1925, and clearly they would've been stored there. But how likely is it that they would've been transferred and reused – and would anyone know?

The Home Front

I find it hard to imagine what the war effort was like; clearly it impacted every aspect of life at the time. My own great grandfather was a docker in Leith and, when war was declared, the docks were shut and he was laid off. There was no money, so he signed up only to find out that that dockers were a protected job and he would have been excluded from any draft. Mind you, as people used to say he had a 'good war', was never wounded and always said the first German he ever saw was at 12:15pm on the 3rd of October 1954, on Leith Walk.

Everyone would have had a serving relative, and in the more industrialised areas there were highly intensive bombing raids. While Stirling famously

Stirling's last surviving air raid siren (280084, 692861; 56° 06 ′ 48 ″ N 3° 55 ′ 48 ″ W)

only ever saw two bombs dropped on it, we still had bomb shelters, Anderson shelters and air raid sirens. The odd bit of graffiti shown above indicates the direction of the nearest bomb shelter, and the strange thing on the side of the building is the last air raid siren in Stirling, right in the heart of storage yards around the railway depot – an obvious target.

But to return to those two bombs, they were both dropped at 2am on the 20th of July 1940. One caused no damage, hitting open ground, while the other destroyed Stirling's football stadium, leaving a smoking crater 18 feet deep and 40 feet wide. The blast radius of this bomb also damaged a row of houses, making several families homeless. The gunner in the bomber also took the opportunity to strafe the town with machine gun fire, and spent shells and bullets were found across the town – one bullet even embedding itself in a church pillar. Rather bizarrely, the bomb blew the door on a nearby joiner's shop off its hinges while the windows remained intact.[147] And in what must surely be a morale boosting tall-tale: a goldfish's tail was blown off and the wee fish was revived from the shock by a few drops of brandy.

Given Stirling's relatively peaceful war, children were evacuated there from Glasgow, including a young German-Jewish girl called Hannah who went to the High School. Rather heartbreakingly, she still supported Germany and later on was detained by the state and interred as a German. Her fate is unknown.

Those who could not fight volunteered in a variety of semi-military functions, the ARP and the Home Guard being the two most famous. The Home Guard trained across Stirling, although there seem to be very few formal records of what they did and where, and so archaeology has a key role to play in locating what they left behind. However, while I have never gone looking for evidence of them, they tend to pop up when I'm doing some-

Dad's army at Abbey Craig

---

[147]   The impact to the joiner's reputation is not recorded, but presumably the glazier enjoyed a surge in sales!

thing else. So far I've recovered rifle casings made in 1942 on Gowan Hill when looking for medieval pottery, as well as dug outs and rock shelters on Abbey Craig (281007, 695673; 56° 08′ 20″ N 3° 54′ 59″ W) when looking for the Early Medieval fort. Intriguingly, a large private house on Abbey Craig was requisitioned to serve as a Prisoner of War Camp for captured Italian officers, all of whom lived in Nissen Huts in the garden ground. These huts were all over Stirling, and there are footings still visible in Bridge of Allan (279322, 697618; 56° 09′ 21″ N 3° 56′ 40″ W) and at the King's Knot near the Butt Well (278962, 693852; 56° 07′ 19″ N 3° 56′ 55″ W).

PENNY MILLAR'S SLAP, CASTLE HILL.

Slums left to rack and ruin: Penny Millar's Slap in the late 19th century (from Auld Stirling Biggins) and today (279161, 693960; 56° 07 ′ 23 ″ N 3° 56 ′ 43 ″ W)

Slum or Heritage

Through the 19th and early 20th centuries, Stirling's population grew from 5,000 in 1801 to 18,000 in 1901 and 27,000 by 1951. There simply wasn't enough decent housing. We have heard of the horrible conditions in the Old Town, and after the war people squatted all over the place – in the Nissen Huts at the King's Knot or in the air raid shelter at Bandeath, where 10 children aged between 1-15 slept on straw over a concrete floor. Others were turned away by Polish soldiers based there, and four adults and ten children walked until 4am to simply keep warm when they then snuck into an air raid shelter. The resulting evictions and prosecutions led 400 men to strike at the Plean pits in protest.

New houses were built at Riverside, Braehead, St Ninians and Cornton, but unfortunately for the Old Town the Council's solution was to remove the older medieval buildings and build from new as there was a slight saving to be made. The demolition process was halted for World War II, but began again afterwards with a regretful passion and zeal. It is estimated that 250 tons of stone were cleared from the town every working day for over seven years.[148] In 1951 a foreign visitor to the city mistakenly apologised, regretting that '*Stirling had been so badly bombed during the war*'. To be fair, this destructive process happened across Scotland at the time, which on reflection perhaps makes it worse.

There were, of course, protests. The *Stirling Observer* used headlines like '*Shovelling Away History*' and a 1948 book, *Old Stirling*, described Stirling as '*a mere shadow of what it might have been. Too much has gone, too much that remains has been mutilated or allowed to fall into decay.*' The Thistle Property Trust (the first in Scotland) was formed in 1928 to buy and restore buildings and managed to renovate 44 buildings, housing 155 people. However, the Council felt it knew better and in a shameful, bullying approach compulsorily purchased all of the Thistle Trust's properties and demolished them.

While we might criticise the Council's approach, ultimately all the people who had lived in the slums were now housed in brand new, warm and dry houses – or as an old woman put it: '*A' ma dreams hae come true for ah've a roof over ma heid and a fire that disna fa on the flair*'.

---

[148]   Some have suggested that the material was dumped next to the King's Knot – right across from what is Stirling's most exclusive street. I mentioned this to someone who lives there, and he spluttered surely not – it would've ruined the view!

Conclusions (and Free Things)

The difficulty with archaeology in Scotland is that in the deep past, Scotland was a poor place on the very fringes of Europe and there's not much to find. So, like many archaeologists, I've focused on the buildings that our ancestors lived in, their forts and houses.

So I was intrigued when Mr Eric Flemming reported finding an inscribed cross on Gillies Hill fort (276866, 691824; 56° 06′ 12″ N 3° 58′ 53″ W). For a fraction of a second I thought of treasure maps and pirates, then early Christians... The next stage was to go and look, and Eric generously agreed to show me on what turned out to be a lovely warm day. The fort had been partially dug in the 1980s and dated to around 300 BC and is always worth a visit. It's a nice gentle

X marks the spot

walk, though with some very rough patches. It's perched on the edge of the cliff with two large ramparts and has a commanding view of the Bannockburn all the way to Earl's Hill; it also glares at another small fort on Lewis Hill above North Third Reservoir.

So what about the cross? Well it's definitely real, carved into one of the ramparts, in the eroded path to the main view point (see if you can find it when you go up). But it's most likely to be from the early Ordnance Survey when they compiled their maps in the middle of the 19th century – a temporary survey station as they measured the country. Ho-hum. So I'll have to keep looking for that treasure – though perhaps we already have it in Stirling's wonderful landscape.[149]

Right, but what about those free things? If I have sparked some level of interest in you but you really don't like my jokes (which is, surprisingly, not all that common), why not head out and use your Right to Roam? You can go anywhere in Scotland that's not a private garden, though of course you shouldn't go through crops or interfere in peoples' businesses. And remember to take your litter with you, keep dogs on a leash and leave the gates as you find them.

The internet can be of great assistance in roaming with the past in mind. Your starting point should be *Pastmap*, which is run by Historic Environment Scotland and is completely free. It maps all that we know and have learned about Scotland's past, and if you know where to look it even features some of my stuff. When you've done that and you want to find out more, try the *Scottish Archaeological Research Framework* and, when you've read all of that, next try the *Society of Antiquaries of Scotland* who have made all of their journals free and online (again, you may spot some of my publications). If you want to read more on Stirling and the Forth Valley then find the *Forth Naturalist and Historian* and read anything and everything by John Harrison and Craig Mair both in and out of the journal. There is enough on these four websites to keep you busy for an entire lifetime.

Thank you for buying the book. I hope that you have enjoyed it and I hope you will visit Stirling, or that – if you already live there – you will be inspired to explore it more closely.

If you want more details of anything in the book (including the sources of the quotes), or you want to come and dig in Stirling, please email me at **cookm@stirling.gov.uk**.

---

[149] Editor to Murray: Really, I must protest; this is far too sickly...

Acknowledgements

THE book was read and edited by the patient Andrea Cook, the multi-talented Therese McCormick (who also did all the line drawings) and the good people at Extremis Publishing.

The photographs are mostly from the author's collection. Thanks to those who provided the other images: Peter Herbert provided the Old Kilmadock Stones and the ruins of the Manse. Nat Theresa and Malkie the Clackmannan Stone. Gemma Cruickshanks provided an image of the Cambuskenneth spear tip. Sue Mackay, the image of the Kaimes Memorial. The Carron cauldron image was by Fiona Buchanan. Historic Environment Scotland let me photograph the lion in Cambuskenneth Tower. The Director of the wonderful Smith Museum and Art Gallery, Caroline Mathers, let me reuse the whale bone image. The Meikle Bin image is republished from Geograph UK under a Creative Commons License (licensed under the Creative Commons Attribution-Share Alike 2.0 Generic license (*https://creativecommons.org/licens-es/by-sa/2.0/deed.en*)) and was taken by Iain Thompson. Finally, the images of Logie Auld Kirk were provided by Joe Young.

About the Author

Dr Murray Cook is Stirling Council's Archaeologist and is from Leith originally, though he also lived and went to school in Edinburgh. He lives in Stirling with a long-suffering wife, three teenage girls and two pesky but loveable cats. He has undertaken numerous excavations across the region and published over 40 books and articles. He won a Stirling's Provost Award in 2018 for his work for the Council, where he has helped raise over £300,000 to be spent on community archaeology and research and has even got invited to see the Queen at Holyrood Palace, along with a few hundred others! He has appeared on several TV programmes, and has sometime even been paid! He writes a regular column in the Stirling Observer and runs Stirling Archaeology a Facebook page dedicated to Stirling's fantastic heritage!:
https://www.facebook.com/Stirling-Archaeology-176144165815143/

Murray studied at Edinburgh University worked first for AOC Archaeology, rising from subcontractor to Commercial Director. His PhD, which has a rather long and boring title, was based on 10 years of research in Aberdeenshire on settlement patterns between 2000 BC and AD 1000:
https://www.scottishheritagehub.com/content/case-study-kintore-aberdeenshire-shining-light-black-hole/

He is an Honorary Research Fellow at Stirling University, a Fellow of the Society of Antiquaries of Scotland, runs an occasional course at Forth Valley College on Stirling and likes to do it in ditches (archaeology that is!). He also co-runs regular training digs open to all under the name Rampart Scotland:
http://www.rampartscotland.co.uk/

A series of recorded lectures by Murray on Stirling's history are available at the Bannockburn House YouTube Channel:
http://www.youtube.com/channel/UC4z6NLizcLmtxpSZ9zph oBg/videos/

Archaeology is at first glance an off-putting word, easy to say but hard to spell and Murray has been called the Council's Archivist and Architect before. But he believes that archaeology should be open to all, it is our shared past and it belong to everyone, so barriers should be removed. On this basis Murray runs a series of free walks, lectures and digs through the year to allow people to explore their past and its open to everyone... email Murray to join:
cookm@stirling.gov.uk

Digging into Stirling's Past

Uncovering the Secrets of Scotland's Smallest City

By Murray Cook

Stirling is Scotland's smallest city and one of its newest. But, strangely, it's also the ancient capital and one of the most important locations in all of Scottish history. If you wanted to invade or to resist invasion, you did it at Stirling. It has witnessed Celts, Romans, Britons, Picts, Scots, Angles, Vikings, Edward I, William Wallace, Robert the Bruce, Edward II, Oliver Cromwell, Bonnie Prince Charlie, the Duke of Cumberland, and even played a decisive role in D-Day.

This huge history has left its mark all over this tiny place. Stirling is Scotland's best preserved medieval city, boasting one of Europe's finest Renaissance palaces, the world's oldest football, Mary Queen of Scots' coronation, James III's grave and murder scene, the site of a successful 16th century assassination of Scotland's head of state, Scotland's first powered and unpowered flights, Scotland's biggest royal rubbish dump, one of Scotland's earliest churches, Scotland's two most important battles, vitrified forts, Scotland's oldest and best preserved Royal Park, connections to King Arthur and the Vikings, Britain's last beheading, Scotland's largest pyramid – and its oldest resident is 4000 years old!

This book tells Stirling's story through its secret nooks and crannies; the spots the tourists overlook and those that the locals have forgotten or never visited. Join Stirling's Burgh Archaeologist, Dr Murray Cook, as he takes you on a tour of a fascinating city's history which is full of heroes and battles, grave robbing, witch trials, bloody beheadings, violent sieges, Jacobite plots, assassins, villains, plagues, Kings and Queens... and much, much more besides.

Exploring the Snow Roads

A Cultural and Historical Companion to the Snow Roads Scenic Route

By David Addison

Starting at Blairgowrie and proceeding through Royal Deeside and the Cairngorms National Park, the 90-mile Snow Roads Scenic Route ends at Grantown-on-Spey. It features the highest main road in the UK and, along the way, it offers the traveller some of Scotland's most spectacular scenery.

What this book seeks to do is to take a look at what lies behind the incredible vistas, to tell the story of the people who once inhabited this ancient landscape, from the Picts to the more recent past.

It's a story with a huge cast of disparate characters. Kings and queens; dukes and duchesses; earls and lairds. Criminals and conmen; chieftains and caterans. Road builders and railway builders; radical ministers and rhymers. Saints and smugglers; storytellers and songsmiths. Jacobites and Redcoats. Pioneers and heather priests.

As testimony to their times, the landscape is dotted with standing stones and stone circles, castles and churches, old military roads and railways, holy sites and battle sites. And associated with them are myths, legends, and folklore – tales galore of love and death and derring-do, murder and ghostly goings-on.

Appreciate the scenery for its own sake, but you will get much more from your trip, see the Snow Roads Scenic Route through more informed eyes, if you read this book first, or take it with you on your travels.

And appropriately enough for a route with snow in its title, the author goes off piste as he visits other places of interest which should not be missed – and where he comes across even more astonishing tales to tell.

The Heart 200 Book

A Companion Guide to Scotland's Most Exciting Road Trip

By Thomas A. Christie and Julie Christie

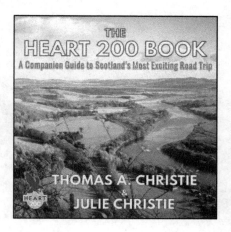

The Heart 200 route is a unique road trip around some of the most beautiful locations in Central Scotland. Two hundred miles running through Stirlingshire and Perthshire, Heart 200 takes its visitors on an epic adventure to suit every taste—whether you are an outdoors enthusiast, an aficionado of history, or simply looking to enjoy yourself in some of the most stunning natural surroundings in the world.

Written with the full approval and co-operation of the Heart 200 team, *The Heart 200 Book* is a guide to the very best that the route has to offer. You will discover the history and culture of this remarkable region, from antiquity to the modern day, with more than a few unexpected insights along the way. Over the millennia, this amazing land has made its mark on world history thanks to famous figures ranging from the ancient Celts and the Roman Empire to King Robert the Bruce and Mary Queen of Scots, by way of Bonnie Prince Charlie, Rob Roy MacGregor, Robert Burns, Sir Walter Scott, Queen Victoria and even The Beatles!

So whether you're travelling by foot, car, motorhome or bike, get ready for a journey like no other as the Heart 200 invites you to encounter standing stones and steamships, castles and chocolatiers, watersports and whisky distilleries... and surprising secrets aplenty! Illustrated with full-colour photography and complete with Internet hyperlinks to accompany the attractions, *The Heart 200 Book* will introduce you to some of the most remarkable places in all of Scotland and encourage you to experience each and every one for yourself. It really will be a tour that you'll never forget.

For details of new and forthcoming books from
Extremis Publishing, including our monthly podcast,
please visit our official website at:

www.extremispublishing.com

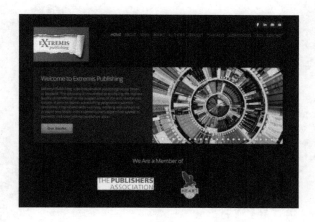

or follow us on social media at:

www.facebook.com/extremispublishing

www.linkedin.com/company/extremis-publishing-ltd-/

CPSIA information can be obtained
at www.ICGtesting.com
Printed in the USA
LVHW080832171120
671844LV00012B/129